LIVING IN HIS LOVE:

ESSAYS ON PRAYER
AND
CHRISTIAN LIVING

LIVING IN HIS LOVE:

ESSAYS ON PRAYER
AND
CHRISTIAN LIVING

BERNARD J. BUSH, S.J.

AFFIRMATION BOOKS
WHITINSVILLE, MASSACHUSETTS

PUBLISHED WITH ECCLESIASTICAL PERMISSION

First Edition

©1978 by House of Affirmation, Inc.

Library of Congress Cataloging in Publication Data

Bush, Bernard J.
  Living in His Love.

1. Spiritual life—Catholic authors—Addresses,
essays, lectures. 2. Prayer—Addresses, essays,
lectures. I. Title.
BX2350.2.B87   248 '.48 '2   78-11809

Printed by Mercantile Printing Company, Worcester, MA
United States of America

Earth's crammed with heaven,
And every common bush afire with God;
And only he who sees, takes off his shoes.
The rest sit round and pluck blackberries.

E. B. Browning
Aurora Leigh

For David T. Asselin, S.J.
(1922-1972)

Who, barefoot, taught many of us that
bushes are never common
and that blackberries are always
more than they appear to be.

CONTENTS

FOREWORD

So many times during our growth in the spiritual life we find ourselves searching for God and the things of God. In this book entitled *Living in His Love,* Father Bush's primary purpose is not to affirm God and spiritual realities but rather to invite us to open ourselves to God's affirmation of our individual personhood as "the apple of His eye." When we live in His love because of desire and not because of fear, life is no longer a mere existence to be endured but is a reality that brings peace and joy and makes our human hearts appreciate the same healing words of hope that Hosea heard: "I am the Holy One in your midst."

I have encouraged my colleague to write two new essays and to make his previously published essays from the British publication *The Way* more available to North American readers. With a rare gift of insight into human and spiritual truths, Father Bush has given us a book that serves not only as material for reflection but as a source to guide us in our friendships with Christ and one another.

I want to take this opportunity to say something about Father Bush. First, he is a fully human and consistently free man. His gentle yet assertive approach to life, his manner and style of affirmation of all that is good, make his pilgrimage on earth as man, priest, psychotherapist, educator, spiritual director, sculptor, and author all very credible.

My Jesuit colleague has guided well the foundation of the second residential House of Affirmation. He continues to be a gift of God to all of us. I hope these words to him and to you convey the fraternal affection, deep respect, and continuous appreciation that I have for him. He lives what he preaches; all of us who have come to cherish him know that Bernie Bush, S.J., is most certainly "living in His love."

I recommend these essays for your careful consideration and prayerful reflection.

Thomas A. Kane, Ph.D., D.P.S.
Priest, Diocese of Worcester
International Executive Director
House of Affirmation

Feast of the Assumption
August 15, 1978

PREFACE

This volume offers a variety of ways of contemplating the life we live. Contemplation is a focusing from the faith point of view on the intersection of the human and the divine. All events in time reveal their full meaning to us only when we become aware of the presence of God in them. Yet the chapters of this book are not instructions in contemplative prayer. Rather they are reflections on how things really are and on the problems we have in becoming habitually aware of God's presence and actions.

The unique source of our understanding of the way God acts in human history is sacred scripture. We have there an unfailing guide to discern what is truly evidence of God's presence and what is not. The problem is that often the language of scripture makes it difficult for us to know exactly what the human experience was of the events described there. In other words, if eyewitness news cameras had been on any of the scenes, what would they have seen? The only conclusion we can reach is that what is described there would have been very much the same as our own mostly ordinary and occasionally extraordinary experiences. The prophetic writers were inspired to call attention to the presence of God in events that may not have been so obvious while they were occurring. The people who hear and believe the prophets are called upon to have confidence that God's activity is continuing in their own lives and times. This confidence must extend equally to us and our times.

The first four chapters of this book were originally published as articles in *The Way,* a quarterly journal of spirituality. The first chapter appeared in July 1970 (vol. 10, pp. 199-210), the second chapter in January 1972 (vol. 12, pp. 20-28), the third chapter in October 1973 (vol. 13, pp. 259-69), and the fourth chapter in July 1976 (vol. 16, pp. 189-98). In addition to the four reprints, I have added two original essays on the topic of community. The title of the book is taken from *The Way* article published in January 1972. It seemed to me appropriate to call the whole volume *Living In His Love* because all the chapters are reflections on our life in God.

It is with the hope that we can all become more aware of God's presence and love in our lives that this volume is offered. After considering and believing that God is with us in many ways, we can then go on to discover in what respects he is calling us out of ourselves to greater fidelity and service.

Although not much is said directly in these chapters about social justice, human rights, or the nearly overwhelming national and international political issues that face us daily, I believe that we are being called by God today to involve ourselves in these issues as an integral part of our faith. Each Christian is called to search his or her heart to find precisely how and when to take action for justice. This volume will have achieved its goal if it increases our faith and confidence in the abiding and inescapably loving presence of God to each one of us. Commitment to action should follow from such faith and confidence.

Thanks are due to the many people who have made this book possible. I want to thank Reverend James Walsh, S.J., editor of *The Way,* for his gracious permission to reprint the first four chapters. I owe Father Walsh great gratitude for his continued interest in and encouragement and support of me personally. It would be hard to express sufficient appreciation to Reverend Thomas A. Kane, Ph.D., D.P.S., International Executive Director of the House of Affirmation, for his consistent affirmation of and confidence in me. Not the least of his virtues is his consistent prodding to write. Among many other acknowledgements that should be made, I would like to name Sister Anna Polcino, S.C.M.M., M.D., International Psychiatric Director of Therapy for the House of Affirmation; Lynnette Perry, Editor of Affirmation Books, who worked long and hard to prepare the manuscripts for publication; and Mrs. Shirley Frediani, the secretary-receptionist at the House of Affirmation in Montara, who showed extraordinary perseverance in typing and transcribing. I also want to express my appreciation to my colleague, Edwin Franasiak, Ph.D. (cand.), whose helpful suggestions always lead to deeper truth and understanding. I have been blessed with many friends, associates, and clients who seem invariably to ask the hard questions and then, together with me, seek the next step toward a solution.

The clients and residents of the House of Affirmation in Montara deserve special thanks because I try out ideas on them and in spirited dialogue we refine some, abandon others, and are frequently led in entirely new and unexpected directions. It was a resident who posed the riddle that I believe sums up much of what I am trying to express about the unfathomable ways of God in our lives: "When does the quest cease to be a question? When it is the answer!"

Rev. Bernard J. Bush, S.J.
Director
House of Affirmation
Montara, California

PRAYER TODAY

PRAYER AND EXPERIENCE

The question of prayer and experience is raised directly by Isaiah when he issues the Lord's summons to conversion: "For my thoughts are not your thoughts, nor are your ways my ways, says the Lord. As high as the heavens are above the earth, so high are my ways above your ways and my thoughts above your thoughts."[1] This is more than a mere assertion of transcendence. It means that God's experience of life is different from our own. Experience is constituted by the judgment, value, and meaning assigned to the events of a life in time. Thus there is a "godly" way of being human and an "ungodly" way of being human. Experience for each type of life will be completely different, not because persons feel things differently, but because they meet them differently. How then are we to arrive at this different experience of being, and what

---

1. Isa. 55:8-9.

19

will be its characteristic features? Isaiah again urges us in the same chapter: "Seek the Lord while he may be found, call him while he is near."[2] So here we have the image of the transcendent ineffable God making himself available to transform the pattern of our thoughts and behavior, that is, our experience, in order to conform it to his own experience of life. This is the promise, and Isaiah says that to attain this *metanoia,* we must pray for it.

What kind of human experience is it that would lead a person to want to trade familiar patterns of life and action for new and unfamiliar, perhaps uncomfortable, ones? Again Isaiah, drawing upon an experience common to saints and sinners, the feeling of inadequacy, assigns it a meaning and tells where it leads: "All you who are thirsty, come to the water! . . . Why spend your money for what is not bread; your wages for what fails to satisfy?"[3] And just so that we do not miss the point and think he is speaking of material food, he adds, "Heed me, and you shall eat well. . . . Come to me heedfully, listen, that you may have life."[4] Any feeling of need can be called thirst or hunger. It might be a vague dissatisfaction with the quality of life in the abundant society, agony over the wars, poverty, exploitation, a longing born of love opening out beyond itself, some personal suffering searching for a meaning, a joy or happiness which one needs to communicate and share. These needs, when assigned their "godly" value, become the origin of a life of prayer and underlie every stage of its progress. Yet even true experience of God, no matter how satisfying, always leads to deeper hunger. "He

---

2. Isa. 55:6.
3. Isa. 55:1-2.
4. Isa. 55:2-3.

who eats of me will hunger still, he who drinks of me will thirst for more."[5]

Our God proves that he is greater than all the other gods in precisely this way. He does not overwhelm us with sweetness and light continually, thus making the other gods less attractive. Rather he has constructed us in such a way that in spite of our efforts we cannot satisfy ourselves or one another with them. He is in truth the hound of heaven, always here, always available, working within us where we experience him as a profound restlessness. We must insist on this, since it is called by all sorts of other names. It is a great temptation to want to explain feelings and personal events in purely natural categories, and hence, experience them as natural or merely human. We even devise bogus remedies, escapes, and anesthetics to cure this kind of experience of God in our life. This is sin in its basic sense, the attempt to fabricate securities without consulting God.[6] St. Paul reminds us: "For all that is not from faith is sin."[7]

CORRECTLY INTERPRETING EXPERIENCE

There is a tendency in some places in the Church today to develop intense interpersonal encounters on deep emotional levels as a way of alleviating anxiety, loneliness, alienation. This can be a vicious circle, since it often leads to even deeper hunger and a search for peace through stronger doses of psychoemotional experience. This has a very seductive appeal to contemporary insecurities raised by the loss of a sense of community. Whatever its origin,

---

5. Ecclus. 24:20.
6. Isa. 30:1ff.
7. Rom. 14:23.

this interior thirst seems quite ordinary, but is really a call from God to drink at the waters of contemplation. It is a personalized call, since the experience of thirst is unique. My need is not the same as anyone else's. The beginning of wisdom is when we realize this and turn to God right there where he is bothering us. "O God, you are my God whom I seek; for you my flesh pines and my soul thirsts like the earth, parched, lifeless and without water."[8] Even sin can lead to God, since it parches the soul. But this kind of understanding is itself a grace and is sheer folly to a person who experiences life in an "ungodly" way. A person who does not feel deep need, who does not realize, however dimly, that the world cannot satisfy him, is dead spiritually. There are simply no gaps for God in his life. He is the one described in Isaiah: "Listen carefully, but you shall not understand! Look intently, but you shall know nothing!"[9] It is also the man pictured in the Apocalypse: "because you say, 'I am rich and have grown wealthy and have need of nothing,' and do not know that you are the wretched and miserable and poor and blind and naked one."[10]

St. Ignatius Loyola in his instructions for recruiting people to make the *Spiritual Exercises* uses the same method:

> Also, when we discover in the conversations they have with us that they are somewhat discontented . . . because they aren't doing so well in their business, or because their parents or relatives don't treat them well or some similar thing; then it can be given them to understand how all men are miserable when they work

8. Ps. 62:2.
9. Isa. 6:9. Quoted in the context of listening to the word by Matt. 13:14.
10. Apoc. 4:17.

solely to satisfy someone other than God, either by riches or other things.[11]

Thus, the call to prayer can come out of any human experience if it is discerned correctly. On the other hand, the habitual and spontaneous mechanisms we employ to handle personal tensions in "sinful" ways can also seem very innocent and natural and are not discerned as temptation. It takes a revelation from God to see our sinfulness *as sin* and not rationalized by some other name. It is a grace that should be prayed for continually, as St. Teresa urges us:

> This must never be forgotten. Indeed I shall repeat it many times, since it is most important. For there is no state of prayer so high that it is not necessary often to return to the beginning, and the questions of sin and self-knowledge are the bread which we must eat even with the most delicate dish on this road of prayer.[12]

Since, therefore, our need before all other needs is to have this faith-vision, Isaiah says that we should seek the Lord while he may be found, and call him while he is near. We should follow the calls of grace when we discover them. This will lead us to a greater interior sensitivity, the desire to assign faith relevancies to our experiences, and to an increased ability to discern the involvement of God in all we think and do. This will mean reordering our human relationships to the extent that they are sinful, and working to become free from all the interior and exterior compulsions which inhibit our ability to find God in our experience.

---

11. P. José Calveras, *Ejercitios directorio, y documentos de San Ignacio* [Autograph directories of Saint Ignatius], trans. Bernard J. Bush (Balmes: Barcelona, 1958), p. 246.
12. J. M. Cohen, trans., *The Life of St. Teresa of Avila* (Edinburgh: R. & R. Clark, 1957), p. 94.

GOD'S WORD WORKS IN OUR LIVES

Prayer at this point becomes a more finely tuned and careful listening to his word with a concomitant desire to respond. This is an obediential listening, and can take many forms and methods. We must listen to God as he tells us what kind of prayer will be most effective. However, all these forms of prayer must be grounded in sacred scripture as the guide in human language of what is authentic in religious experience. If we meet any other god than the one described there, he is a false god. Yet this listening is not without its own problems. When we let the word into our lives, it begins its own work. The scriptural models for this are many, but all contain a warning to our self-sufficiency. Isaiah says: ". . . so shall my word be that goes forth from my mouth, it shall not return to me void, but shall do my will, achieving the end for which I sent it."[13] The letter to the Hebrews: "For the word of God is living and efficient and keener than any two-edged sword, and extending even to the division of soul and spirit, of joints and of marrow, and a discerner of the thoughts and intentions of the heart. And there is no creature hidden from his sight."[14] The Psalmist: "The voice of the Lord strikes fiery flames!"[15] Jeremiah: "Is not my word like fire, says the Lord, like a hammer shattering rocks?"[16] Then there is the parable of the sower, which is a fundamental paradigm of the degrees and conditions of obediential listening.

By thus taking the living word of God into ourselves, we

13. Isa. 55:11.
14. Heb. 4:12-13.
15. Ps. 28:7.
16. Jer. 23:29.

will be transformed into his image. We will be putting on Christ who is himself the perfect image of the Father. We will have in us that mind which was in Christ Jesus.[17] This requires a willingness constantly to be undergoing a revision and replacement of cherished values and securities. There is simply nothing outside of God that can be the point of self-definition. All dimensions of achievement—intelligence, knowledge, personality, social relationships which include the deepest bonds of human love and friendship, even apostolic successes—can be obstacles to union with God. That is, whatever a man uses as landmarks to define and locate himself, or to secure his self-esteem and gain respect from his fellow men, will be the purest vanity if they are not transformed and integrated by Christ. This is deep freedom and is not to be presumed too easily: the chances for self-deception are very great here. We must continually pray for liberation from these very sophisticated forms of slavery to the world. St. Paul describes his experience of this replacement: "But the things that were gain to me, these, for the sake of Christ, I have counted loss. Nay more, I count everything loss because of the excelling knowledge of Jesus Christ, my Lord."[18] This knowledge which is experiential rather than conceptual produces the change of affectivity, so that whoever prays comes to prefer what Jesus preferred, to see the world the way he saw it, to love what he loved, to hate what he hated, and to suffer and die in imitation of him. To be Christian, then, and to live joy, peace, and love, means allowing Christ to take over my experience and lead me through his own. Christian community will be the assembly of those

---

17. Phil. 2:5.
18. Phil. 3:7-8.

who believe and share the same experience. Our *koinonia,* community, is "the fellowship of his sufferings; become like to him in death, in the hope that somehow I may attain to the resurrection from the dead."[19] Or, as Jesus describes it, "But you are they who have continued with me in my trials."[20]

PURIFICATION FOR FREEDOM AND PEACE

This work of interior transformation can be distressing because it can seem as though everything has been taken away without anything to replace it. This is the desert or dark night experience. Many souls beat a hasty retreat from this phase, not because it is so terrible, but because it seems so neutral and vague. We have had a taste of the transfiguration joy, a foretaste of the resurrection, and are very reluctant to rejoin the Lord, "Jesus only," and the companionship of the long dusty road to Jerusalem. Our life with the Lord is much of the time like Peter who recognized him and loved his company, who received revelation and prophesied without even knowing it, but still kept one ear cocked for the values of the world. "And Peter, taking him aside, began to chide him saying, 'far be it from you, O Lord; this will never happen to you.'"[21] This ambiguous witness is characteristic of too many of the Lord's disciples who are still scandalized at the cross. More accurately, we are not scandalized at the cross "out there" where it adorns the walls of our houses, but rather that this annoyance, this irritation, this insult, this grievance could be the cross offered to me. Christ's reaction is swift and

19. Phil. 3:10-11.
20. Luke 22:28.
21. Matt. 16:22.

pointed: "But he, turning and seeing his disciples, rebuked Peter, saying, 'Get behind me, Satan, for you do not mind the things of God, but those of men.'"[22] Anyone who wants to live close to Christ must be willing to endure such rebukes—even welcome them. This kind of obediential listening causes pain in resistant flesh. Jesus, who became sin for our sake, is given to us as sharing this experience; "And he, Son though he was, learned obedience from the things that he suffered."[23] For our part, we can expect the same thing, for "God deals with you as sons; for what son is there whom his father does not correct? . . . Now all discipline seems for the present to be matter not for joy but for grief; but afterwards it yields the most peaceful fruit of justice to those who have been exercised by it."[24]

And so the purpose of all the purification is peace and the increased ability to hear the word of God gently stirring in our hearts. After the rocks are broken by the mighty wind, the earthquake and the fire, the Lord speaks to us in the gentle breeze.[25] Occasionally this happens in experiences which can only be called transcendent—infusions of light, love, understanding—a vision in faith of the reality of God which is simply beyond the spectrum of the merely human and is understood to be such. At other times it may be very hard to discern the hand of God in some event or circumstance, but he is always there directing us, as Isaiah reports: "The Lord will give you the bread you need and the water for which you thirst. No longer will your teacher hide himself, but with your own eyes you shall see your

---

22. Mark 8:33.
23. Heb. 5:8.
24. Heb. 12:7; cf. Deut. 8:5.
25. 1 Kings 19:11-12.

teacher, while from behind, a voice shall sound in your ears: 'This is the way; walk in it,' when you would turn to the right or to the left.''[26] We must reflect prayerfully on every aspect of our lives in order that all our experience be Christian experience.

CHRISTIAN COMMUNITY FOUNDED IN PRAYER

We have a basic desire to want to increase, to be created, to grow, become wise, to act creatively. Everyone points to the reality that this can only be accomplished in some kind of community. We find ourselves when the "I" and the "thou" become a "we." Thus we are most truly constituted ourselves when we accept that we are loved and hence lovable. This is how we locate ourselves; and when this dimension is absent, we are lost. But here again, because of the facts of change, suffering, and death, we are always conditionally constituted. No matter how good it is, we know that it is not going to last. As Rev. John Sheets, S.J., has observed: "We were not made to share a common humanity but to share that for which a common humanity provides the foundation—a sharing in the life of the Son.''[27]

It is this desire to share the Spirit of Christ that is leading many Christians to a desire to share the experience of prayer itself. They range from the enthusiastically pentecostal to quiet gatherings sharing scripture reading. The unity and love that characterize these groups bears a different "feeling" from groups gathered for any other purpose. There is explicit orientation to the Father as the point

26. Isa. 30:20-21.
27. Rev. John Sheets, "Four Moments of Prayer," *Review for Religious* 23 (May 1969), p. 397.

of definition for the relationships in the group. The perfect expression of this prayer is seen to be the liturgy of the Eucharist, where all enter into sacramental unity with the offering of the life of the Son to the Father. In this experience, which gathers the meaning of every aspect of our lives, personal and social, we can always locate ourselves because the Spirit in us is always turned to the Father: "For if I do not go, the Advocate will not come to you; but if I go, I will send him to you . . . when he, the Spirit of truth has come, he will teach you all the truth . . . whatever he will hear he will speak."[28] Jesus, the one who baptizes with the Spirit, thus fulfils the prophecies of the new creation when men would be interiorly directed by an entirely new principle.

When we pattern our lives on the sacred scriptures, they will then shape our expectations of what is truly creative and authentic in our manifold relationships. They will shape the way we love. At this point we must seriously accept that if we are to love as Christians, we must love as Jesus loved. This will cost us our life, our radical selfhood, as it cost him his. It reverses all the natural expectations of how love is to be experienced. The simple fact is that the death of Christ is the paradigm of love in the new creation. Also contrary to natural expectations, the experience of the death of Christ in us is joy-filled. St. Paul says, "for as the sufferings of Christ abound in us, so also through Christ does our consolation abound."[29] This is the major theme of his writings, stemming from his encounter with the risen yet still-suffering Lord on the road to Damascus:

---

28. John 16:7-13.
29. 2 Cor. 1-5.

"I am Jesus whom you are persecuting."[30] The action of calvary is not over and done with but is a continuing experience in the Church and in each member.[31]

UNITY IN THE LOVE OF CHRIST

Hence in the Christian scheme, the consummation and fulfilment of love will be to share the experience of Christ's love. In the first place, it will be the *kenosis,* the act of love whereby he emptied himself to enter our history. So love will be an emptying rather than a filling, a giving rather than a getting. Any loneliness can be an experience of this kind of love. Our supreme experience of love will be when we share his supreme experience of love, where he said "it is consummated." To share this experience with the Lord is the reason why mystics long for death, and martyrs die in ecstasy. It is not a desire to escape from the tedium of the world, or of relations with other persons, but is a burning desire to embody the peak experience of Christ's love in themselves. They become impatient with the daily cross, the partial, progressive embodiments of his death in themselves. Here it is necessary to be careful not to deny that the desire to be in heaven with God, our Lady, the saints, and angels as a state preferable to this one is praiseworthy. The fourth Eucharistic Prayer expresses it thus: "Then, in your kingdom, freed from the corruption of sin and death, we shall sing your glory with every creature through Christ our Lord." St. Paul describes Christ's sacrifice as love and speaks of his own progressive entrance into it, looking forward to his own death: "But God proves his love for us,

---

30. Acts 9:5.
31. Cf. Col. 1:24ff.

because when as yet we were sinners Christ died for us."[32] Further, "With Christ I am nailed to the cross. It is now no longer I that live, but Christ lives in me."[33] And with great longing, "For to me to live is Christ, and to die is gain . . . desiring to depart and to be with Christ, a lot by far the better."[34]

This view of life and love considerably modifies human relationships. As the Lord predicted, it will destroy some and rebuild others.[35] It is, however, not something that can be assimilated or worked out intellectually. It is a conviction produced in us by the action of God in our souls. The means to attain it is to pray for it, consistently, insistently. We must beg for our own death and transformation. As Hans Urs Von Balthasar observes:

> In contemplation . . . one has to look the word in the face, feel God's gaze fixed upon one, and, in acknowledging him to be right, condemn oneself. That is one of the main reasons why people so persistently avoid contemplative prayer, and, though admitting its necessity in principle, evade any personal encounter with the word.
>
> It is quite impossible to contemplate the word if one does not seriously intend to let it influence one's conduct . . . anyone who practices contemplation must have the courage to face the word, the sharpness of the sword and the burning fire.[36]

This talk of suffering and death may sound threatening and beyond normal Christian experience or perhaps simply traditional. Yet it is important to have realistic expecta-

---

32. Rom. 5:8.
33. Gal. 2:20.
34. Phil. 1:21.
35. Cf. Luke 12:49ff.
36. Hans Urs Von Balthasar, *Prayer,* trans. A. V. Littledale (New York: Paulist Press, 1967), pp. 176-77.

tions of what prayer leads to in our lives. We must have a correct "feel" for what is genuine Christian religious experience. To affirm that suffering and death are the distinguishing characteristics of love *as Christian* is necessary in the light of the current temptation to see sex as the highest expression of human love. This is not gross or crude. There can be a subtle idolatry of marriage when the martial union of love is valued as the highest and the most creative experience of love. The phallic symbol of love is pagan. The crucifix is its replacement in the new creation. Yet many desert Calvary for the home and hearth in the name of Christian creativity: "I have married a wife, and therefore cannot come."[37]

We cannot extort happiness or joy or fulfilment from God on any other than his terms. And his terms are seen in Christ who emptied himself to share our emptiness and to make it redemptive. "For you know the graciousness of our Lord Jesus Christ—how, being rich, he became poor for your sakes, that by his poverty you might become rich."[38] Thus by his cross and resurrection he transforms the consequences of our sin—existential poverty, radical alienation, suffering, and death—into the means of salvation. He did not exempt us from the necessity of experiencing these things, but he infused them with hope, that is, with his living resurrected presence. Identical feelings can lead to different conclusions. "For the sorrow that is according to God produces repentence that surely leads to salvation, whereas the sorrow that is according to the world produces death."[39] Hence, concomitant with ac-

---

37. Luke 14:20. The excuses are many: cf. Luke 9:59ff.
38. 2 Cor. 8:9.
39. 2 Cor. 7:10.

cepted suffering, persecution, misunderstanding, real injustice, struggle with sin, minor and major irritations, will be faith, hope, deep peace, and, dare we say, love, joy, and happiness. This polarity of reactions to personal suffering and its relationship to Christ's cross is typified by the two thieves crucified with him. One wanted to use Christ to escape from the pain. He saw only the absurdity of enduring something unpleasant if it could possibly be avoided or anesthetized. The other accepted the suffering as the consequence of his sin, superimposed it on the cross of the only one who really suffered innocently, and saw paradise the day he did it.

HUMAN EXPERIENCE HAS DIVINE MEANING

The most creative moment in history, when sin was destroyed and the new creation began, was the moment of Christ's death and glorification. This moment will define and judge all other creativity. It was the moment when Christ definitively and irrevocably entered human history as human, never again to be driven out, and made himself available to every man now. From the very core and center of life, he challenges each one personally: Do you want a share of the action? Will you enter the new humanity?[40] Will you drink the cup?[41] Will you continue with me in my trials?[42] Will you love one another as I have loved you, and lay down your life for each other?[43] Are you willing to enter entirely new patterns of kinship, not related to natural bonds of affinity, by hearing the word and acting

40. 2 Cor. 5:17.
41. Matt. 20:22.
42. Luke 22:28.
43. John 15:12-13.

upon it, thus becoming my mother, brothers and sisters?[44]
Will you do your good before men in such a way that they
will give glory to the Father and not to you?[45] It is a life of
discerning the pattern of the supernatural in the natural. It
means a life of consolation, peace, tranquility. It is the
freed love described by St. Ignatius in his definition of consolation in the *Spiritual Exercises*:

> I call it consolation when some interior motion is caused
> in the soul whereby the soul comes to be inflamed with
> love of its Creator and Lord; and consequently when it
> is able to love no other created thing on the face of the
> earth in itself, but only in the creator of them all.[46]

Again and again, Jesus uses human encounters and experiences as the occasion to reflect upon their real meaning. For example, he corrects the woman from the crowd
who expressed a purely natural view of his relationship to
his mother. He said, "Rather, blessed are they who hear
the word of God and keep it."[47] He discerns the work of
his Father in the capacity of his disciples to make sense of
his words and uses it as an occasion for prayer: "I praise
you, Father, Lord of heaven and earth, that you hid these
things from the wise and prudent, and did reveal them to
the little ones . . . and no one knows the Son except the
Father."[48] So when Peter recognizes the Son and blurts
out his confession of faith, Jesus discerns the presence of
his Father and is at pains to instruct him that what has just
occurred is not recognition according to merely human
ways of knowing one another: "Blessed are you, Simon-

---

44. Luke 9:21.
45. Matt. 5:16.
46. *Spiritual Exercises,* 316.
47. Luke 11:28.
48. Matt. 11:27.

bar-Jona, for flesh and blood has not revealed this to you, but my Father in heaven.''[49] This meaning was apparently not a self-evident experience to Peter. We have already seen what happened when Peter recognized him simply according to the ways of men. Finally, Jesus often provides commentary on the meaning of what is occurring by citing relevant portions of the psalms and prophets. He does this especially during the passion where the chances of misunderstandings are greatest.

We find the same kind of reflection in Mary, who "pondered these things in her heart." Her understanding of the visitation, as given to us by Luke, shows her communicating the word before he was even born. She transmitted him through an "ordinary" greeting and act of charity. Elizabeth provides the discernment. Her joy was caused by the presence of the Lord in the person of the "mother of my Lord."[50] In St. Paul we have a similar reflection, explicitly attributing to God the consolation experienced through the joyful encounter: "For indeed when we came to Macedonia, our flesh had no rest; we had troubles on every side, conflicts without and anxieties within. But God, who comforts the humble, comforted us by the arrival of Titus."[51] Perhaps it is more difficult to recognize God in experiences of joy than of suffering.

AWARENESS OF SINFULNESS

In addition to growth in charity—"the way Jesus loved"— and the ability to discern the hand of God in every human experience, another hallmark of true progress

---

49. Matt. 16:17.
50. Luke 39:45.
51. 2 Cor. 7:5-6.

in prayer will be increased awareness of personal sinfulness. The saints often speak of themselves as the world's
greatest sinners. This testimony is not pious pretension or
exaggeration. It is uncompromising truth, deriving not
from introspection or heightened psychic sensitivity, but
from the revelation of God. It is the soul being shown itself
as God sees it, sinful, lost, being graciously loved and
redeemed. Only God can produce this understanding in the
soul because only God knows what sin really is. This
awareness does not therefore precede the entry of God into
my life, but is its first and continuing effect. It is the experience expressed by Peter when he said, upon realizing
the presence of God, "Depart from me, for I am a sinful
man, O Lord."[52] His vocation to follow the Lord pro-
ceeded from that moment. St. Paul reflects the same conviction when he says: "This saying is true and worthy of
entire acceptance, that Jesus Christ came into the world to
save sinners, of whom I am the chief."[53] He is describing a
unique experience. It is self-revelation with an entirely personal character. The sinful soul before God in prayer is not
just one of a fallen race, more or less equally guilty, but
"me." It is "my" sin that is revealed. If the person begins
comparing his sin with others, he gets told about the beam
and the mote. St. Gregory the Great has a famous dictum
about this: "The sun turns brown him whom it touches
closely; so the Lord, when he comes, darkens him whom
he most touches by his grace, for the closer we come to
grace, the more we recognize that we are sinners."[54]

---

52. Luke 5:8.
53. 1 Tim. 1-15.
54. St. Gregory the Great, *Supra Cantica Canticorum expositio,*
PL 79, col. 486; cited in François Roustang, *Growth in the Spirit*
(New York: Sheed & Ward, 1966), p. 150.

If prayer is sustained and the living word is allowed to penetrate to the sources of my life, changes of the sort described will inevitably occur. The time to worry is when a person seems to be praying and nothing is happening. Often the problem is simply that one is reading, studying, thinking, or doing any number of things except the real confrontation which is prayer. Talking about prayer and reading articles on the subject are no substitutes for doing it.

The Vatican Council, reflecting on life's goals, and the quality of experience which makes it Christian, urges:

> Only by the light of faith and by meditation on the word of God in whom "we live, and move, and have our being" (Acts 17:28), seek his will in every event, see Christ in all men whether they be close to us or strangers, and make correct judgments about the true meaning and value of temporal things, both in themselves and in their relation to man's final goal."[55]

The growth of this awareness in our hearts will cause the promise given through Isaiah to be fulfilled in us. "Yes, in joy you shall depart, in peace you shall be brought back; this shall be to the Lord's renown, an everlasting imperishable sign."[56]

---

55. *Apostolicam Actuositatem,* 4.
56. Isa. 55:12-13.

PRESENCE

LIVING IN HIS LOVE

When Jesus first encountered his disciples, their question to him was, "Rabbi, where do you live?" His reply was "Come and see."[1] In a similar way, the purpose of this article is to come and see where Christians love. For Christian love is first of all an environment. It is the place where we "live and move and have our being,"[2] the interior life of the Trinity. Moreover, along with the rest of creation, our place within this Trinity is in the second person. There St. Paul locates us when he writes:

> He is the image of the invisible God, the first-born of all creatures. In him everything in heaven and on earth was created . . . In him everything continues in being.[3]

Hence the place where we live with him is in him. And it is

---

1. John 1:39.
2. Acts 17:28.
3. Col. 1:15, 16a, 17b.

there that we will live in his love, sharing the eternal life of love, the Holy Spirit. "God chose us in him before the world began, to be holy and blameless in his sight, to be full of love."[4]

To love as Christians, we must have an abiding consciousness that our life is in the Trinity—and that it is their life and love that flow through us. It is here that our relationships both to God and men originate. We relate to God from within him, and to one another as sharers in the same life and love.

Yet we live our lives in a material universe of time and space. So we do not see the God who contains us and loves us. On the contrary, we see much that is not God, but is in fact visible resistance to life and love. We feel forces of evil and deterioration. We have them right within ourselves, where they struggle for ascendancy.

> Yes, we know that all creation groans and is in agony even until now. Not only that, but we ourselves, although we have the Spirit as first fruits, groan inwardly while we await the redemption of our bodies.[5]

In our fallen human condition we are in the Trinity, but not of the Trinity.

Naturally speaking, in our present state there would be no hope of our bodies ever being permeated by the love of God since they are of themselves incorrigibly resistant to God. But there is a body wholly possessed by the Spirit which is capable of absorbing our own. The body of Christ, through baptism and progressive purification, is precisely the place where we lose our God-resistant life to live with his life. To live in the Trinity now means to be

---

4. Eph. 1:4.
5. Rom. 8:22-23.

there with all our humanness, since it is part of the humanity of the second person himself. And conversely, our life in the Trinity is a life that is incarnate in this world, at this time.

Thus locating the place where Christians love is essential for an understanding of how we are to experience and express this love in our lives. First of all, it allows us to describe the encounter in which this love becomes a transforming reality within us. Secondly, it gives us a basis for understanding the nature of Christian community. Thirdly, it makes it possible for us to list the ingredients of any genuine expression of love. And finally, it provides a framework for dealing with the obstacle to love that is fear.

WE MEET GOD IN THE FLESH

St. John tells us that we know that we live in the Spirit when we can acknowledge that Jesus Christ has come in the flesh.[6] Encountering Christ in the flesh, therefore, is the experience that leads to growth of his life and love within us. And this encounter takes place as we come to recognize him through the various modes of his presence: in the Church, the sacraments, through contemplation, and in the mystery of Christian community. Thus we meet him primarily in the Eucharist. Here he penetrates our being with his self-sacrificing love. We take him within our bodies in order that he might more fully incorporate us into his own, drawing us visibly into his Church. We also meet him through contemplation. When we become quiet to pray, we experience his presence within us. It is a real presence, sometimes consoling, sometimes reproving,

---

6. 1 John 4:2.

always challenging, always moving us beyond ourselves to share his presence in us with our neighbor. We are filled with his life when we listen in a receptive way to God's Word in the scripture. And if the word finds a home in us and rings true with our whole being, we know that our flesh is becoming more and more conformed to the flow of life, love, and truth which is the dynamism of the Trinity—where we are.

Then it is that we experience, deep within ourselves, peace and understanding of the mystery which is real in us but which we cannot see except by faith. For the recognition of Christ is never according to the ordinary ways of human experience. As St. Paul says regarding our life in Christ:

> Because of this we no longer look on anyone in terms of mere human judgment. If at one time we so regarded Christ, we no longer know him by this standard.[7]

If we are to live in his love, then, it is necessary to live by faith. It is necessary to see ourselves in a relation to the persons of the Trinity and to let this vision define our relationships to one another. Any failure in love reveals a lack of this faith-perspective about who and where we are—a failure in contemplation.

COMMUNITY BASED ON SHARED FAITH-VISION

Christian community stems from lives based on this perspective. It is a way of life built upon vocation and grace rather than upon natural compatibility. Christians find it in their hearts to love their enemies, to be at the service of all men with constant fidelity. Their love is a committed love, which endures for life and through death itself. It is a

---

7. 2 Cor. 5:16.

struggling love, which shows its power in overcoming the forces of sin and despair. No obstacle is too great for it to overcome. No evil, interior or exterior, can crush it. It never gives up. It finds strength to laugh in the midst of tears. It can be sorrowful, repentant, joyful, and hopeful all at the same time. For Christ's love in us, born of faith and carried on in hope, is the foundational experience of a new life within. Although it is a transcendent love, it is one which we find within us in a deeply mysterious way. It is not on the level of emotional reaction or transitory like and dislike, but is much deeper than all of these things. It is more like awe and humility, as my deepest self (where I dimly sense myself to be immortal) touches the same place in another. Inviolable bonds are forged there, and only faith can know their meaning. St. John describes this love in his first letter:

> Love, then, consists in this: not that we have loved God, but that he has loved us and sent his Son as an offering for our sins. Beloved, if God has loved us so, we must have the same love for one another.[8]

God is the source of all love; and the community which lives in this love shows that it is based, not on our more limited ways of loving, but on the gift of his eternal love in us. The Christian family, for instance, manifests the presence of this kind of love. Although the union may have originated in a natural, mutual attraction, deeper roots of love must be discovered if it is to endure. The children given to the parents may not be the ones they would have chosen, but they love them as grace from God. Religious communities too show divine love when they are formed, not merely by natural affection or bonds of compatibility,

---

8. 1 John 4:10-11.

but by the common recognition that God has selected and called this group of people to aid one another to grow in his love and to show this love to others.[9] Community is founded on, and grows in, mystery. It flourishes to the extent that its members understand the mystery through prayer, the sacraments, and mutual spiritual edification.

This kind of community can exist even in the midst of evil. This is so because living in his love does not rule out the possibility of sin and failure. They are the inescapable consequences of being members of the race of Adam. What it does require is that sin be recognized for what it is and not called by some other name. It is in fact the presence of his love that reveals, and causes us to recognize, our sinfulness. The discovery of sin is the first effect of God's entry into our lives.[10] He works this recognition at the heart of our being, where he touches us and draws us back through faith and hope to the source of love, there to be met by forgiveness.[11]

CHRIST'S PRESENCE TRANSFORMS

In all these ways, Jesus, the second person of the Trinity incarnate, brings us to resonate more and more perfectly with divine love in our human condition. Living in his love means letting him come to life in us. And if we thus live in union with him, he will show us how to live the reality of divine love in our own lives. We must expect that this will go contrary to our natural expectations, sometimes severely and painfully so. Christ's love in us will make us small in men's eyes, and the one who would be the greatest will be

---

9. Cf. Matt. 5:16.
10. Cf. Luke 5:1-10; also Isa. 6:5.
11. Cf. Luke 15:17-20.

humbled until he is the least. Although He has led the way, we will encounter a great deal of unconscious, and often unsuspected, resistance to recognizing this as one of the effects of living in his love. Yet "the way we came to understand love was that he laid down his life for us; we too must lay down our lives for our brothers."[12]

One of the first effects of this presence of Christ's love is a devotion that leads to a kind of single-mindedness. The heart ceases to be divided.[13] The praise and worship of God, and the readiness to do his will, now become the central concerns in a person's life. They are central because God's love has become the very center of his life. And, as we suggested earlier, there is the recognition of the same presence at the very center of every other man's life. Contemplating this reality at the heart of our lives gives rise to a peaceful love that draws all our concerns and relationships into a unity, the human within the divine.

Thus the love that flows from the presence of God's Son in our midst is also deeply reverent. It is a love that knows how to respect the dignity, integrity, fragility, and commitments of the other. I then love them the way God loves me because I see God in and through them. This means that I relate to people with tenderness and delicacy and genuine affection—not merely seeing them as those who need help or those who can help me. It means that I give and receive love by really taking the other within myself and allowing myself to dwell in him. "By obedience to the truth you have purified yourselves for a genuine love of your brothers; therefore love one another constantly from the

---

12. 1 John 3:16
13. Cf. Matt. 6:21-24.

heart."[14] This reverent taking of the other within my purified heart, where constant love now dwells, makes me an agent of redemption and salvation for him.

> Be imitators of God as his dear children. Follow the way
> of love, even as Christ loved you. He gave himself for us
> as an offering to God, a gift of pleasing fragrance.[15]

GROWTH IN LOVE

Another essential ingredient of the love that exists among Christians is patience. All the emotional, erotic, or unstable aspects of love must be drawn into the patient self-sacrificing core and heart of divine love. This is not to deny the validity of these lesser loves, but to deny them the autonomy to seek their own private ends. Control is the soul of love and enlivens it with the quality of fidelity. This is hard for the present age to accept. The "now" genera-tion (and that includes all of us) wants instant love of perfect union without the asceticism of suffering and wait-ing. Yet love needs time to mellow before it can acquire gentleness and tenderness, which are signs that it is inte-grating all the forces of the personality. And this is always a slow process, since it requires the purification of our competitive and aggressive tendencies. It requires the re-nouncement of the personal securities and positions of safety from which we manage and manipulate our relation-ships with others. It requires a humility that will depend on God's grace to direct and fashion our love where we can-not do it for ourselves. And it requires a willingness to have our sinfulness and our egoisms exposed. This is the service Christians render one another when they love in

---

14. 1 Pet. 1:22.
15. Eph. 5:1-2.

spirit and truth. They do not simply help the other to "think positively." They do not merely suggest that he "cheer up because things will get better." For this would be simply to confirm the other's impatience. Rather, their love is an encouragement to die well—which is the same as to live well. There is continual challenge to conquer the more immediate and noisier clamorings of selfish love—to let redemptive self-sacrificing love take possession. All of this, of course, takes time and prayer.

Christian love thus leaves us vulnerable to many forms of suffering. These are part of the experience of love itself, and yet can be recognized as such only from the perspective of faith.

> We are afflicted in every way possible, but we are not crushed; full of doubts, we never despair. Continually we carry about in our bodies the dying of Jesus, so that in our bodies the life of Jesus may also be revealed.[16]

The dying of Jesus in us is our share in his love.

This suffering will make its appearance even in the way in which Christians show their love. For one thing, the love of the Lord's disciples will be based on the divine wisdom which is always foolishness to this world. Thus it will strengthen a chastity which has been integrated into the whole personality and which joyfully accepts to live within the limits imposed by existing commitments: to the commandments, to spouse, or to vows.[17] This joyful accep-

---

16. 2 Cor. 4:8-10.
17. We will find that love always implies stages of commitment, which (if they are to be genuine) must not assume more responsibility than they can bear. There are sexual ways of expressing love, for example, which characterize the permanence and union of Christians within marriage, but which are not genuine outside marriage because they imply degrees and qualities of commit-

tance of restraints and obligations does not imply the absence of tensions in such living. We are imperfectly integrated. But tension and pain, which result from the need for patience and reverence, will be recognized as part of love as He lives it in us. "If we are children, we are heirs as well, heirs of God, heirs with Christ, provided we suffer with him so as to be glorified with him."[18] Even Christ had to make his "flesh" obey through struggle. "Son though he was, he learned obedience from what he suffered; and when perfected he became the source of eternal salvation for all who obey him."[19] The process of learning to love will be the same for us.

In this way even the endurance of loneliness can be a fruitful sign of Christian love and a part of commitment to eternal love. Insofar as a kind of loneliness is attendant on every sort of love in this world, it is a suffering to be united to his. And the fruit of such suffering is deepened love. Thus St. Paul encourages the Romans:

> We know that affliction makes for endurance, and endurance for tested virtue, and tested virtue for hope.

---

ment that can be borne only by marriage. For those vowed to love in a characteristically different way, the words "I love you" will have the same qualities of permanence and union. But affection will be manifested in ways which unambiguously declare that the commitment to love is in a different mode. It is true that humans need to experience love from other humans as well as from God. And it is true that genuine affection cannot be expressed in a sterile, "formalized" fashion. Yet guidance and personal spiritual direction are absolutely necessary here if Christian love, in any given relationship, is not to degenerate into the lowest forms of human need-fulfilment. The death of love is the use of others for personal fulfilment.

18. Rom. 8:17.
19. Heb. 5:8.

And this hope will not leave us disappointed, because
the love of God has been poured out in our hearts
through the Holy Spirit who has been given us.[20]

FEAR IS AN OBSTACLE TO LOVE

Our difficulty is that we instinctively fear the suffering that
is always a part of love.

Fear and love, however, are mutually incompatible, as
St. John tells us:

Love has no room for fear; rather, perfect love casts out
all fear. And since fear has to do with punishment, love
is not yet perfect in one who is afraid.[21]

So fear is an obstacle to love. Yet fear is commonly the
reaction of the heart to the intrusion of love. It can arise
from many sources. It can be fear that my life will now get
out of hand because there is an element of the unpredict-
able about love. It is a threat to my customary patterns of
thought and action. It is a commitment continuing through
an uncertain future.

We also tend to fear that in loving another person we
may subtract from the love that we owe to God. Of course,
this can be a real difficulty, since there are ways of showing
human love which are incompatible with loving God. We
sometimes want to take the bride to ourselves, instead of
realizing that the Lord is the bridegroom—whose voice
and presence should make our joy full since we have been
waiting there, listening for him as he comes to take possession.[22] In other words, we sometimes draw off love to

---

20. Rom. 5:3-5.
21. 1 John 4:18.
22. John 3:29. John's profound humility consisted in his understanding, "I am not the messiah; I am sent before him" (John
3:28), as must ours.

ourselves which properly should be directed to God. And yet fear of this must not become a motive for staying aloof, distant, "professional." We are commanded to love one another, and in fact we are told that the love we have for one another will be a sign of the fact that we love God.[23]

The movement of love is to return to its source, drawing all things with it. Hence loving one another in his love will inevitably draw us into a deeper appreciation of God our Father, who is merciful and forgiving and whose name is love. His Spirit takes possession of us to accomplish this from within:

> All who are led by the Spirit of God are sons of God.
> You did not receive a spirit of slavery leading you back
> into fear, but a spirit of adoption through which we cry

23. John 13:34-35. Cf. also 1 John 3:23 and John 15:17. As we have pointed out, in the arena of love it is impossible to intellectualize and thus manage either ourselves or others. That is why love, the authentic and the false, must be understood and disentangled by the discernment of spirits rather than by conceptual or ethical schemes. Moreover, no discernment is possible where the requirements of God's love are not put ahead of all other personal interests. The criteria by which we can determine whether it is God's Spirit that is dominant in a person's life are gathered succinctly in the fifth chapter of the Epistle to the Galatians. Here St. Paul observes that "those who belong to Christ Jesus have crucified their flesh with its passions and desires" (24). Since the love of God does not flow perfectly freely through us, when it meets resistance it produces disturbance within. This can be a saving experience as God's love becomes a purifying fire in the soul. Only after attachment to sin has been removed can discernment proper take place, because only then is there desire for progress in love and responsiveness to the Spirit. It is then that a person can learn to distinguish the promptings and impulses of the diverse spirits by the characteristic feeling they produce within the heart.

out, "Abba!" (that is, "Father"). The Spirit himself gives witness with our spirit that we are children of God.[24]

Yet for his children in this life, the Spirit of love leads us to the Father through Christ's death, resurrection, and ascension into glory. Those who love God and one another in Christ, therefore, meet on Calvary, where this love is found in its purest human form. Again, this reality remains incarnate in the Church, where we meet at the Eucharist to be the community present at his dying and rising. There we grow in love by feeding it with his body and blood, the sacrament of divine love. So we are drawn, as redeemed humans, into the mystery of his life in the Trinity, where we share unlimited love.

UNIVERSAL HUNGER FOR CHRISTIAN LOVE

This kind of love is what the world is looking for. It is dying to hear the words "I love you" in a way that is convincing and consoling. The words must go from heart to heart and have a ring of the eternal about them. They must come through as though spoken by God whose covenant with each of us is unbreakable. The scepticism about love these days is largely the result of conditional promises and temporary, provisional commitments. This scepticism most often reveals itself as either sentimental romanticism or cynical brutality. We need a sign of love that exists in time but endures for eternity. Such a sign of love is Jesus on the cross, his promise that was kept. For "stern as death is love, relentless as the nether world is devotion; its flames are a blazing fire."[25] The world must be able to see

24. Rom. 8:14-16.
25. Cant. 8:6.

that a Christian commitment of love is not going to mean something different tomorrow because conditions have changed, or because loving may no longer be convenient or secure, or because suffering has entered the scene.

One indication in our times that this experience of God and love within the community is what many are seeking has been the spreading interest in charismatic renewal in the Church—the so-called pentecostal movement. This movement supplies for many an experience of enthusiastic, zealous Christianity and the sharing of transcendent love. This phenomenon, along with others that could be cited, points to a need in the Church for the kind of love we have been describing.

Thus there is the continual movement of God's love within each of our lives, a creative action which calls our being into a unity. In this movement we live more and more deeply in the heart of the life of the Trinity—their love, where we must truly meet one another. "As the Father has loved me, so I have loved you. Live on in my love."[26]

---

26. John 15:9.

SACRED AND SECULAR

EXPERIENCE OF GOD

God reveals himself in words that men can understand. He comes to us in time and space, in movement and process. He meets us in our world with its concerns and problems, its good and evils. The accordion-like movement of God's action, compressing and extending through history, calls us to correspond with his will by consolidating or stretching in unison with him. The sign, therefore, of authentic personal experience of the living God is the conformity between what we hear him saying to us in our hearts and what he reveals externally through the signs of the times. This union of faith and action is made difficult because it occurs in that realm where we find ourselves hard of hearing and dim of vision, if not deaf and blind, and sluggish in response.

This chapter will explore with a developmental systems model some characteristics of God's call in our age, and some of the difficulties in response that man is presently meeting.

God first revealed his typical way of calling his people to movement when he said to Abraham: "Go forth from the land of your kinsfolk and from your father's house to a land that I will show you. . . . Abraham went as the Lord directed him, and Lot went with him. Abraham was seventy-five years old when he left Haran."[1] The key to understanding this passage, for the purposes of this chapter, is given in the Epistle to the Hebrews: "By faith Abraham obeyed when he was called, and went forth, moreover, not knowing where he was going."[2] Now, if there is anything that is predominant in the signs of our times, both in our personal lives and in our historical movement, it is that we are painfully, acutely aware that we do not know where we are going. God allowed Abraham seventy-five years of consolidation, and then abruptly called him to extend himself from Haran into darkness. It was radical, unexpected, and made him reach beyond reason to faith. He did not know where he was going, and that call to trust was, for Abraham, the hallmark of the authenticity of his experience. These dimensions of Abraham's vocation are also true in our times.

God reveals himself as a God of process, of time and history. He calls for a trust that is absolute and utterly personal. He says to each: "I who love you will care for you, and I want your love for me to show itself by trusting dependence, and by going to the place that I will show you." Hence the experience of God is in fact an ongoing

---

1. Gen. 12:1-4.
2. Heb. 11:8.

series of experiences, each one of which must be left behind in order to meet him anew. Since life with God means living and moving with him, the relationship will be accompanied by a kind of continual grieving for the loss of God, as well as by the continual temptation to settle into any one experience and call it final. This temptation is especially strong after the first encounters with God, which seem so wonderful and full of the promise of repose and fulfilment. Then somehow we find ourselves alone, perhaps confused, and wondering if the meeting were real at all. If we are faithful, we can grieve over the loss of God, knowing that there is no turning back, no recapturing the bliss of Haran or Tabor; and we can go forth again.

CONVERSION IS A CONTINUOUS PROCESS

We have just been describing the process of conversion, or *metanoia.* It is a process that extends over time and is experienced in many different ways with varying degrees of intensity or vagueness; but the rhythm is the same for every person who meets God and for the community of man as a whole. It is God himself who has revealed that this is the way he will meet us.

The process of experience of God is analogous to the progressive stages of human development, from learning basic trust to intimacy, union, and interdependence. Each stage must be assimilated, lost, grieved over, then combined with all the previous stages so that it becomes the base for further integration. If a person gets locked into any one stage, or regresses to previous more comfortable and apparently more secure positions, growth stops and a pathological condition develops. For example, when a child is learning to walk, the mother holds him while he takes his first steps. A relationship is formed within which the child feels very supported and secure. Then the mother steps back, and the child feels bewildered and abandoned. Doubt and a sense of betrayal are very real. If the child takes several steps by himself, he can come to understand that his mother has faith in his ability to walk by himself. Confidence grows and the child believes that he is trusted and can trust the care of his mother in a period of extension when he is without the previous support. For a while the mother catches the child before he falls and a new dependency grows. However, a time comes when the child is allowed to fall, and again the sense of betrayal and loss of protection occurs. Part of this process of growth is learning that all is not lost by a mistake. A new level of confidence and trust should emerge from the experience when it has been reflected upon and accepted. Similarly, we progress through life consolidating gains, losing, grieving, trusting, gathering all past experience, and extending. There is no stopping. Moreover, all of these aspects of the growth-process go on simultaneously on different levels. So we are at the same time losing in one respect, grieving over something else, and consolidating some gain. On the spiritual level, for instance, we are both grieving over the death and loss of Jesus and rejoicing in his resurrection. There is no rest unless a person chooses to stagnate psychologically or spiritually. The iron law of development is that it is through leaving behind, a kind of dying, that we come to life.

When God possesses the memory, growth comes out of encounter and departure. St. John of the Cross speaks of this purification of the memory as necessary so that the faculties of the soul may focus on the action of God.[3] All the elements of distrust must be progressively removed so that the soul may grow in intimacy with God. St. Ignatius describes the same process in the rules for the discernment of spirits in the *Spiritual Exercises*:

> . . . let him who is in desolation labor to hold on in patience . . . let him consider that he shall soon be consoled. . . .
>
> . . . let him who is in consolation think how he shall carry himself in the desolation that will come on afterwards, gathering new strength for that time.[4]

This is the language of process and of the confident acceptance and anticipation of growth through alternating experience.

The psalmist is continually praying in the same manner. He recalls the wonderful deeds of God in the past, knows that he cannot go back to them, affirms his belief in the hidden action of God in the present, and hopes for the future. God himself, through Isaiah, cries out against the idolatry of settling down in any facet of the relationship with him: "Remember not the things of the past, the things of long ago consider not. See, I am doing something new! Now it springs forth, do you not perceive it?"[5] God is speaking here of himself in the language of faith-in-process. One of the reasons that the mystics have such a hard time describing their experience of God is that they are aware of the impossibility of trying to capture a love relationship that is constantly evolving, and for that reason is dark and inexpressible. A cloistered nun recently described her personal experience of this same reality:

3. *Ascent of Mount Carmel,* bk. 3, chaps. 1-15.
4. *Spiritual Exercises,* 318, 320-23.
5. Isa. 43:18-19.

If one takes days as a whole together they seem much alike, but how many myriads of tiny differences from one to another. So it is, I guess, with my soul: myriads of nuances of his love intertwined in each moment, and yet the general aspect seems much the same.[6]

GOD CALLING US THROUGH THE PROPHETS OF OUR TIME

God demands both of the individual and of the community that they set out on the journey and leave the conversion experience behind in order to be aware of the "myriad nuances." The signs of this call to the world today are also myriad. Many prophetic voices are calling for a more radical public witness of our commitment in the form of true poverty, labor for peace, and self-sacrificing charity to the poor of God. Insistently in recent years, the magisterium of the Church has called to the rich nations to dispossess themselves of the affluence they enjoy because of their oppression of the poor. We believers are being called to join all men of good will to reform the sinful structures of our society. Here again is the voice of the prophet calling upon Israel to cease oppressing the poor, the orphan, and the widow. This call is being made in the name of God, and is a strong indication of the direction he is taking. Nations or churches or persons who profess to be serving God today must seriously examine what God they are following if they do not hear or heed the prophets' voices, or if they even help to silence or to dilute these voices.

God's vocation to us is as radical and unreasonable as the demand he made to Abraham to give all away and go to a new land. Such a summons can be heard only where

6. Correspondence with Discalced Carmelite, March 2, 1973.

there is faith and an unwavering commitment not to rest in
an autistic complacency or a false confidence inspired by
our previous experiences of God's love for us. The disciples could have remained on the mount of the transfiguration, but if they had, they would have found it a sterile,
barren place, because God in the person of Jesus had gone
forth in commitment to serve his people, to walk the long
dusty roads to Jerusalem and his death. He had been
strengthened by the experience on Tabor, but he did not
rest there. In fact, he even told the disciples to forget about
what had happened until later, when they would be better
able to remember and see it in the context of history and
process. The process is always the same: grieving over the
loss of God, commitment of service to his people, redis-
covery of God, risk of death, hope in the resurrection.
There is no room for nostalgia for the past experience.
God is a God of the here and now. He is the giver of daily
bread. He condemns the man who hoards his riches. That
contemporary prophetic voices are almost universally ignored is to be expected when one considers the unhappy
history of God's appeals to his people. However, today the
voices are not being ignored in some sectors of the third
world, among the poor themselves, who look in amaze-
ment at those of us who are in a position to do something
but who are not moving; and yet we all claim to be listening to the same God.

UNITY AND BALANCE OF ALL REALITY

A disturbing voice is also being spoken in the expression
of those men of our age who often profess not to believe in
God, but who are seeking the unity of mankind in thought
and in action. This humanitarian striving sounds very

much like a prophetic call. Conscious of the interrelatedness of all phenomena, modern thinkers are taking a
systems approach to problems rather than isolating and
considering the parts individually. Solutions are being
sought in terms of ecological balances and *gestalts* in the
attempt to remedy deviations in the functioning of the systems. In living systems such as the human, the being func-
tions on many levels simultaneously and is a member of
many interacting systems. For example, a man is a finely
balanced biological system with many subsystems all exer-
cising a mutually causal effect on each other. A deviation
in any one of the parts of the system influences all the
other parts. In fact, the deviation cannot be properly
understood separated from its influence on the other parts,
and its being influenced by them. It is clear that men who
are working to improve the human condition are eagerly
calling upon all the sciences to provide their perspectives
for a more integrated view of the system of the world.
Those who have faith in God believe that he is the ultimate
system, the unifying force of all reality. From a systems
point of view, the words of St. Paul sound very scientific
as well as mystical:

> In him, everything in heaven and on earth was created,
> . . . all were created through him, and for him. He is
> before all else that is. In him everything continues in be-
> ing. It is he who is the head of the body. . . . It pleased
> God to make absolute fullness reside in him and, by
> means of him, to reconcile everything in his person,
> both on earth and in the heavens, making peace through
> the blood of his cross.
>
> God has given us the wisdom to understand fully the
> mystery, the plan he was pleased to decree in Christ, to
> be carried out in the fullness of time; namely, to bring

all things in the heavens and on earth into one under Christ's headship.[7]

Hence men who are thinking and working to solve many world problems are being led toward the knowledge of God through their ever-expanding reflections on unifying systems. While they may say that a believer's private experience of God is only of marginal importance to their main concerns, and may even be held suspect, a cosmic yet intensely personal awareness of God is quite intriguing to them. These men are aware that there are intimations of a transcendent unifying principle in the purposefulness of natural systems and their mutual interdependence. It is the task of believers to translate these intimations into realities on the levels of theory and practice.

A prophet in this age, as in every age, is one who can interpret the signs of God's action in time into language that men can understand. The prophet's message will have credence to the extent that he can combine true knowledge of men, their needs, and their language, with God. Yet, since the prophet is not himself in a static state, his awareness of himself is that of one who is committed to process in relation to others who are also in process. He knows that he must move because he has been called by God to move, and because he is in relationship to other men who must also move. He is a conscious member of the people of God, which is a pilgrim community.

CHRIST'S MYSTICAL BODY: A UNIFYING SYSTEM

The analogy of the mystical body is apt here. It is a symbol of an integrating, unifying system in which part cares

---

7. Col. 1:6-20 and Eph. 1:9-10.

for part, while at the same time the whole is living, growing, changing, and doing. What scandalizes men and makes it hard for them to believe in a dynamic God is the example of a body that is neglecting itself. Then it is a system out of balance, where deviance seems to predominate. It is a body in which some parts are indulging themselves at the expense of other parts. The witness of the rich members of the body of Christ feeding off the poor members calls into serious question the authenticity of the experience of God, at least in the lives of the rich members. The consequences of this kind of systems thinking are radical and seem to converge with the way God moves, if we take scripture as a norm. Ezechiel, especially, was called upon to perform symbolic countercultural actions to call Israel's attention to its unfaithfulness.

The real effect of a prelate being driven in his own limousine to a news conference to protest abortion, while another part of the body is starving in the streets of Latin America because of the system that has provided the prelate with the car, is incalculable in this day of the global village. Socially and politically his protest is nullified by his insensitive example. Spiritually, the situation is a traumatic insult to the mystical body; that is, it is sin. It is not enough to say that the sign does not have to go where it points. Such an attitude betrays a lack of commitment to and unity with the process of the system. In short, to harbor this attitude is to separate oneself from God, who is no longer in the expected place, but who has moved on. The image of the prelate is used to accentuate the point. In fact, the whole community and each of us in it are being called to examine ourselves and to give living prophetic witness. Those who seem to be speaking most clearly to these issues, in addition to the magisterium of the Church, are the theologians of the third world who are laboring to develop a theology of liberation.

> . . . the new theological thinking now occurring in Latin America comes more from the Christian groups committed to the liberation of their people, than from the traditional centers for the teaching of theology. The fruitfulness of reflection will depend on the quality of these commitments.
>
> If we look more deeply into the question of the value of salvation which emerges from our understanding of history—that is, a liberating praxis—we see that at issue is a question concerning *the very meaning of Christianity.* To be a Christian is to accept and to live—in solidarity, in faith, hope and charity—the meaning that the word of the Lord and our encounter with him gives to the historical becoming of mankind on the way towards total communion.
>
> The product of a profound historical movement, this aspiration to liberation is beginning to be accepted by the Christian community as a sign of the times, as a call to commitment and interpretation.[8]

Conversion at the core of a person's being is the basic experience of the believer. It is an experience that changes the heart from stone to flesh.[9] It is a call heard in faith which demands that the hearer "give all away in order to come and follow." The test of the genuineness of the call coming to the Christian community from so many sectors is the similarity of our reactions to those disciples of Jesus: "Then Jesus looked at him with love and told him, 'There is one more thing you must do. Go and sell what you have

8. Gustavo Gutierrez, *A Theology of Liberation* (New York: Orbis Books, 1973, pp. 102, 49, and 35.
9. Ezech. 36:26.

and give to the poor. . . . After that, come and follow me.' At these words the man's face fell. He went away sad, for he had many possessions.''[10] If salvation is bound up with liberating praxis in the context of historical process, as cited above, the response must surely be: "Who then, can be saved? To which he replied, 'Things that are impossible for man are possible for God.'''[11] There is an essential note of conflict to the call which is often noted in the Gospels, and almost as often quickly passed over. "I have come to light a fire on the earth. How I wish the blaze were ignited! I have a baptism to receive. What anguish I feel till it is over! Do you think I have come to establish peace on earth? I assure you the contrary is true; I have come for division.''[12] The conflict within man comes from our attachment to the familiar and secure and from our timidity in the face of what seem excessive and unreasonable demands.

CALL TO ACTION WITHIN THE SYSTEM

It is important that the agents of conversion understand and be committed in faith to process and development. In the language of general systems:

> . . . the survival of any living system (here defined as any self-maintaining entity, from closely bounded units like the cell to loosely bounded units like the family) depends on two important processes. One is morphostasis, which means that the system must maintain constancy in the face of environmental vagaries. It does this through the error-activating process known as negative feedback; the simple house thermostat is usually given

---

10. Mark 10:21-22.
11. Luke 18:26-27.
12. Luke 12:49-51.

as an example. The other process is morphogenesis, which means that at times a system must change its basic structure. This process involves the positive feedback loops and is deviation amplifying, as in the case of a successful mutation which allows a species to adapt to changed environmental conditions.[13]

Since man is free and master of his own change, understanding the signs of the times and reflecting prayerfully on the movements of the Spirit will enable the agent to determine how in any given period and level of structure he is being called upon to act. Thus, on the levels of consolidation he will act in a deviation-countering way, and on the levels of extension he will act as a catalyst of change in a deviation-amplifying way. Both these processes can be at work simultaneously in the same agent on different levels with respect to person, community, nation, church, or globe. The adage that "all that is needed for the triumph of evil is that good men do nothing," that is, maintain the status quo, is an example of how deviation-countering activity on the wrong level can in fact be sinful. God is asking us to become aware of changed environmental conditions, to discern his call in and through them, and to act as agents of our own liberation in truth. Jesus speaks of himself as the true prophet and agent of historical development. "Lord, said Thomas, we do not know where you are going. How can we know the way? Jesus told him: 'I am the way, and the truth, and the life.'"[14] Jesus speaks directly to the issue of truth and liberation from sin in the context of Abraham: "If you live according to my teaching, you

---

13. Lynn Hoffman, "Deviation—Amplifying Processes in Natural Groups," in *Changing Families,* 1971, p. 290.
14. John 14:5-6.

are truly my disciples; then you will know the truth and the
truth will set you free.''[15]

It follows that some of the currents of modern spirituality should be looked at closely in the light of what has
been said. There is, for example, a rapid growth in the
popularity of privately directed retreats. Rising from this
experience is the deeply felt need for ongoing spiritual
direction to consolidate and extend the fruits of the retreat.
This direction is necessary, since, as St. Ignatius says in the
eighth rule for second week discernment:

> . . . the spiritual person . . . ought to look with much
> watchfulness and attention to discern the proper time of
> such actual consolation from the following, in which the
> soul remains aglow and favored with the flavor and
> remnants of the consolation that is past: because often
> in this second period, by her own proper activity, work-
> ing upon habits and consequences of concepts and judg-
> ments, she comes, either through the good spirit or
> through the evil spirit, to form various purposes and
> opinions, which are not given immediately by God our
> Lord; and therefore they must needs be very well dis-
> cussed before entire credence is given to them and they
> are carried into effect.[16]

THE PROBLEM OF A PRIVATIZED SPIRITUALITY

It is in the period after the retreat when one is on the
level of spiritual consolation that the temptation exists to
''privatize'' the experience and to cling to the spiritual
''turn-on'' of the retreat. There is evidence that this situation is actually happening. It is a temptation to a call to a
species of spiritual complacency that baptizes the status

---

15. John 8:31-32.
16. *Spiritual Exercises,* 336.

quo of a plentiful life with a secure future basking in the glow of God's sanction. It should be kept in mind all the time that the majority of our brothers live in circumstances of life so precarious that they do not even have the leisure for the luxury of any kind of "spiritual" experience. A citation from a theologian of liberation, referring to ecclesiastical and political dysfunctioning systems, can apply equally to a similarly dysfunctioning interior life when the parts are out of balance.

> It is interesting to note that when there was no clear understanding of the political role of the Church, the distinction of planes model [strict separation of spiritual and temporal] was disapproved of by both civil and ecclesiastical authorities. But when the system—of which the ecclesiastical institution is a central element—began to be rejected, this same model was adopted to dispense the ecclesiastical institution from effectively defending the oppressed and exploited and to enable it to preach a lyrical spiritual unity of all Christians. The dominant groups, who have always used the Church to defend their interests and maintain their privileged position, today . . . call for a return to the purely religious and spiritual function of the Church. The distinction of planes banner has changed hands. Until a few years ago it was defended by the vanguard; now it is held aloft by power groups, many of whom are in no way involved with any commitment to the Christian faith. Let us not be deceived, however. Their purposes are very different. Let us not unwittingly aid the opponent.[17]

A purely "privatized" spirituality, then, can have disastrous effects in the mystical body and can hinder justice in the world. On the level of privilege alone, it is evident that there is high prestige accruing to those who are in the van-

---

17. Gutierrez, p. 65.

guard of the retreat, spiritual direction, discernment of spirits, and charismatic movements. Those who are being lionized should be very much on their guard against being seduced away from proclaiming the harsher realities of the Christian life. On the other hand, the spiritual-political activists and those who are insistently calling for radical reform, even revolution, of the oppressive structures of our society may be personally admired even though they do not have much institutional support. As long as they remain on the fringe of the Christian community they remain showpieces to the world, the "token" radicals of the Church.

Let us suppose for a moment that a retreatant made a directed retreat and told his director that his meditation of the Two Standards had led him to the conviction that he should take radical political or social action against the unjust social structure of his country. What would the director's reply be? We might find a clue in the directions of Ignatius to the retreat director. Since Ignatius felt that religious life was a more radical way of living the Christian commitment than marriage, and therefore safer for salvation, he said that clearer signs from God were required for the retreatant to make an election for marriage than for religious life.[18] Hence, *mutatis mutandis,* greater indications of the spirit might be required for the less radical change than for the greater.[19]

---

18. Program to Adapt the Spiritual Exercises, *Autograph Directories of Saint Ignatius Loyola,* p. 8.

19. Cf. Spiritual Exercises, 189: "For the amendment and reformation of one's own life and estate." The section ends with the words: "For let each one reflect that his advancement in all spiritual things will be exactly in proportion to the degree in

CONCLUSION

We have seen that experience of God entails in this age, as in every age, the process of progressive detachment and setting forth into the unknown. This personal pilgrimage is a passage through the stages of growth in trust toward the union of intimacy in love. Continuity is provided by the memory, the agent of faith-guided reflection, which shows us that God's action is evolving, not static. The same function is served for the community by the prophet. A systems theory is one model for understanding levels of personal and community faith-involvement in the world. This model provides a point of convergence with modern thought, and can be used to describe the mutual interdependence of social systems and structures and the mystical body of Christ. The model also gives direction to considerations that input on one level has effects on other levels as well. Prophets' voices as well as the magisterium of the Church are calling on believers to take a world view in which political and social structures are interdependent. Spirituality, concerned with the experience of the relationship between God and man, must take these calls seriously as the authentic signs of God's action in the world pointing the direction for believers to take. In the words of St. John:

> I ask you, how can God's love survive in a man who has enough of this world's goods yet closes his heart to his brother when he sees him in need? Little children, let us love in deed and in truth and not merely talk about it.[20]

---

which he goes out from self-love, self-will, and self-interest.''
Cf. also 337-44, "Rules for Almsgiving"; and 351, the sixth of the "Rules for Scruples."
20. 1 John 3:17-18.

THE HEALING COMMUNITY

HEALING GRACE

Since I undertook to write this chapter on healing grace in the light of our experience at the House of Affirmation, I have been listening with particular care to the troubled religious men and women who come to us. What follows is my attempt to articulate some reflections on my experience of that mysterious, mutually shared process of healing which takes place in the context of faith and therapy that is our ministry. I will give a brief outline of the history and work of the House of Affirmation and then add some observations on professional Christian life and personal identity as it is evolving today. Particular attention will be paid to those aspects of contemporary religious living that present themselves through our clients as areas causing or intensifying psychological problems. It is not my intention, however, to deal extensively with the various psycho-pathologies we treat, as this is a chapter on spirituality rather than a discussion of psychology as such. There is a danger of oversimplification when making comparisons drawn from clinical experience with disturbed persons to religious life as a whole. Yet the people who come to us are from so many places in the world and from so many different types of communities and congregations that I feel justified in making some limited generalizations.

We are living in an age of rapid transition in which there is evidence of both decay and growth. We can find abundant reasons for despair and for hope. It is only by listening carefully with a discerning ear to all the evidence available that we will be able to understand what the Lord is saying to us. It is my belief that the people who are hurting and confused have at least as much to say about what is happening in the Church and world as those who are seemingly contented. There is often an incisive candor in a person who is suffering that cuts through to the sensitive heart of the matter.

Within the week prior to this writing, I have heard the following statements from sisters, priests, and brothers of various communities. (The quotations in this chapter from clients are printed with their permission.)

> Living in a ninety-eight percent female environment is so sterile. I yearn for, no I am so lonesome for, real life.

> My rectory is antiseptic. The formalities are observed, but day in and day out, I never meet—I don't know what I am saying, but it is so. O hell! It's dead there, and I'm dead too.

> I have such a gut aloneness, that I don't know what to do or where to turn.

> Somehow I just can't shake the fear. I'm afraid all the time.

My superior is kind, and tries so hard, but I just can't stop being afraid of him, and, in fact, I'm afraid of anyone in authority.

I don't find community a vital life-giving experience.

I deep down don't have confidence in my sisters. I always feel like they are judging me.

No matter what I do I feel guilty. Even if I please everyone else, I can't seem to please myself. I am a worthless failure.

I am coming more and more to resent celibacy. I don't know what it means. Not that I want to get married, I don't—and I do so want to serve God and his people, but something is so deeply missing. There is this man who loves me. We haven't done anything wrong, but I'm tempted to because it's only when I am with him that I really *feel* like I am loved. My sisters say they love me, and I suppose they mean it, but it just doesn't somehow feel real.

Statements such as these, which are quite typical and taken at random, provide a source for reflection on religious life as it is actually being lived day to day. The people who said these things to me are not the malcontents or misfits. In each case they were said by religious who are functioning and holding positions of responsibility. They are considered in some instances to be the happiest and most stable members. What shows is not always what is really going on. Religious are exceptionally well trained to keep the cheerful front and to avoid looking at the realities. Communities often encourage such pretense. Some clients say that they dare not reveal to their communities what they are really thinking and feeling, or even that they are coming to us for help.

The obvious reply to what I have said is that of course we all have our moments of loneliness, sadness, depressions, and doubts, but is that not just part of the life we have chosen? Why dwell on that? Is there not enough misery around? The reasons for hope and confidence, the signs of the redeeming hand of God, abound. It is easy to point out the faults and failures. It takes greatness of vision and faith to build up rather than to tear down. Why must we be continually reminded of the depressing side of religious life?

THE MINISTRY OF THE HOUSE OF AFFIRMATION

It is the unique ministry of the House of Affirmation to the Church to ask these questions and to search out the truth in order to heal and reconcile in an atmosphere of renewal and love. Our community is an international therapeutic treatment center for emotionally troubled religious and clergy. It began in 1970 as the Consulting Center for Clergy and Religious for the Diocese of Worcester, Massachusetts. The original outpatient service expanded in 1973 to include a residential treatment facility in Whitinsville, Massachusetts. Since then two additional satellite outpatient offices have been opened. In 1974, I opened an office in Boston, and Sister Malachy Joseph Lynch of the Selly Park Sisters opened one in Birmingham, England, in 1975. Then, in 1977, Edwin Franasiak, Ph.D. (cand.), and I opened a second residential facility in Montara, California. Plans are now underway for a third residence in the Midwest. This expansion was made in response to the ever-increasing demand for our services. Each move was sanctioned and welcomed by the local diocesan and religious superiors. However, the House of Affirmation is a non-profit organization, incorporated in the Commonwealth of Massachusetts. Its relationship to the Church, while not official, is close and collaborative. It is entirely dependent for its material functioning on donations from interested foundations, concerned members of the laity and clergy, and from donations made by communities and dioceses whose members come to us.

The variety of programs offered by the House of Affirmation includes individual and group therapy, communications and growth groups, career and candidate assessment, consultation to religious communities and workshops on psychotheological issues, an internship leading to a master's degree in clinical psychology, creative potential development courses, and an inservice training institute for formation personnel.

The founders of the House of Affirmation are Sister Anna Polcino, S.C.M.M., M.D., and Reverend Thomas A. Kane, Ph.D., D.P.S. Sister Anna, formerly a missionary surgeon in West Pakistan and Bangladesh, is a practicing psychiatrist. She is presently the psychiatric director of therapy. Fr. Kane is a priest psychologist of the Worcester Diocese and is executive director of the House. Both have impressive academic, religious, and human qualifications for this work. Since its founding, the clinical staff has been increased as the need for expansion arose. This includes psychologists, psychiatrists, art therapists, and a psychiatric nurse. There is additional part-time staff who provide the ancillary therapies which fill out the program. We also have a dedicated staff of housekeepers, cooks, administrators, and maintenance people. The staff is as widely varied as the Church itself, with diocesan and religious priests, brothers, sisters, and lay persons, married, single, and widowed, men and women of all ages and several cultures. Many schools of psychology are represented, as well as widely diversified educational backgrounds and interests.

The staff and residents together make a unique religious community within the Church. The atmosphere at the New England residential facility is familial and dignified in a beautiful eighty-year-old mansion and neighboring buildings in the rolling hills of Massachusetts. There are twenty-five people in residence, which is the maximum capacity. The residence in California is situated in lovely natural surroundings. It is four blocks from the ocean, surrounded by hills, fifteen miles south of San Francisco. Fr. Kane aptly describes these facilities as places for the treatment of the whole person in a wholly therapeutic environment.*

ATMOSPHERE AND TREATMENT

The House of Affirmation is a total therapeutic milieu with one permanent community and one which changes. In

---

*For fuller historical and biographical information and more detailed descriptions of different aspects of our work, I refer the reader to the published writings of our staff: Sr. Anna Polcino, M.D., ed., *Intimacy: Issues of Emotional Living in an Age of Stress for Clergy and Religious* (Whitinsville, MA: Affirmation Books, 1978); Rev. James P. Madden, ed., *Loneliness: Issues of Emotional Living in an Age of Stress for Clergy and Religious* (Whitinsville, MA: Affirmation Books, 1977); Rev. Thomas A. Kane, *The Healing Touch of Affirmation* (Whitinsville, MA: Affirmation Books, 1976); Rev. Bernard J. Bush, ed., *Coping: Issues of Emotional Living in an Age of Stress for Clergy and Religious* (Whitinsville, MA: Affirmation Books, 1976); Sr. Gabrielle L. Jean, "Affirmation: Healing in Community," *Review for Religious* 34 (1975), pp. 535-41; Sr. Anna Polcino, "Psychotheological Community," *The Priest* 31 (September 1975), pp. 19-23; and Rev. Thomas A. Kane, "The House of Affirmation," *Brothers Newsletter* 17 (1975), pp. 18-27 and *Who Controls Me?* (Hicksville, NY: Exposition Press, 1974).

order to ensure a healing atmosphere and a climate of loving cooperation, the staff devotes considerable attention to its own interpersonal relationships. Time is regularly scheduled for the staff to meet to discuss clinical issues, enjoy one another socially, share areas of expertise, pray, resolve the inevitable conflicts that arise, and supervise one another. Care is taken that each staff member stays in good health and gets proper recreation. Decisions that affect the life of the community are arrived at by discussion and consensus. Thus the atmosphere among the staff is one of openness and shared responsibility. It seems that this human dimension, carefully attended to, is at least as important as clinical expertise for the work of healing, since it serves as a model of healthy community living. We are generally happy, hopeful, caring men and women of deep faith and love for the Church.

Our treatment philosophy, as the name implies, is affirmation of the whole person. Affirmation is the positive response to the recognized goodness of the other. It is an experience of a kind of relationship that is creative of the person. The opposite of affirmation is denial, or nonrecognition and nonresponse to the other. The effect of denial is psychic annihilation. Nonaffirmed persons have generally experienced deprivation of affection in childhood, which is later reinforced by the impersonality and task-orientation of religious life. When personal worth is unrecognized and unacknowledged by others, the religious comes to believe that he or she has no value. The nonaffirmed person can go through the motions of a productive life and even outwardly look happy, but much of the appearance is pretense. Inside there is anxiety, fear, insecurity, feelings of worthlessness, and depression. Efforts to boost oneself and reassurances from others do not seem to touch the deeper core where the unrest lies. Such feelings then produce behavior which is self-defeating, such as attention seeking, physical complaints, excessive busyness, hostility masked by a "cheerful" facade, addictions, futile attempts to please others, conflict with peers and authorities, and compulsive sexual acting-out. Such behavior serves only to increase loneliness and guilt-laden depression.

These problems are not cured by intensified spiritual practices or facile reassurances that one is OK, but by the genuine love of another which is felt and makes no demands. Such unqualified love creates a nonthreatening environment where the person feels secure enough simply "to be." An atmosphere of consistent affirmation gives the necessary personal space and freedom to each person to develop his or her human identity as the base on which to build religious and community identities.

PROBLEMS OF IDENTITY FOR RELIGIOUS

Every person is constituted by an almost infinite variety of identities. Each one partially answers the question, "Who am I?" These identities are arranged interiorly by each person in a constantly shifting hierarchy of relative importance. The identity which at any given time is the most personally important receives the greatest amount of attention and energy. There are, however, some identities which are of greater intrinsic value than others. For instance, my family and name are intrinsically more important for knowing who I am than is the color of my eyes. Both, however, are constitutive of my total identity. In the case of many religious, the relative value which is assigned to various identities is not in conformity with their real value. It is not uncommon to find religious professionals who find their most significant personal identity through membership in a particular congregation. This identity by affiliation is followed in order of importance by priest, sister, brother, function; then by Roman Catholic, Christian, nationality, man or woman, the least important identity being one's humanity. Thus the objectively least important ingredients of personal meaning become the most important to the individual and receive the most cultivation and attention. In fact, until recently, the most important and basic elements of personal identity, namely, humanity and sexuality, were considered evils to be overcome. How can grace build on nature when one's humanity is deficient? It is much easier, but personally devastating in its effects, to define oneself in terms of a role than to rejoice in the goodness of being a living person. In other words, there are fairly accurate ways of measuring oneself and thus knowing when one is behaving like a "good" religious of a particular congregation, or a "good" sister or priest, because the criteria are constantly being spelled out objectively in documents or group customs. It is much harder to know when one is being a "good" human, or a "good" man or woman. This problem of personal priority of identities becomes more acute when the various identities are seemingly in conflict. A man finds who he is as a man in relationship to his complement, a woman, and vice versa. However, when the atmosphere of seminary, convent, or rectory is so restrictive that it prohibits or discourages normal relationships with the opposite sex, sexual identity must be developed in relation to the same sex. This exclusiveness often contributes to mutual reinforcement of the worst aspects of masculinity/femininity and impedes the process of maturing. Finally, when one's identity is defined in terms of observance of rules and structures, and those rules and structures are called into question or changed, the person who is unsure of his or her more basic identity experiences an acute emotional crisis. Some of the signs of such crisis are feelings of anxiety, bitterness, scepticism, defensiveness, selective rigidity, and awkwardness in situations that call for human responses rather than pat dogmas.

Religious professionals have been uniquely trained to be models of the perfect life with ready solutions to the mysteries of this and the after life. But we who once thought we were already in the promised land are now finding ourselves once again wandering around in the Sinai desert. We simply do not have the roadmap. The familiar landmarks of devotion have disappeared. However, we do have the special perspective of faith, the indispensable and unique point of departure for reflection to be shared with our fellow pilgrims. We are partners in a dialogue with the world, immersed in its life and profoundly sharing its questions and doubts. For this task, the religious person should be first a sound human being, striving for maturity in the normal human way: that is, through the development of progressively deeper personal relationships and friendships. Faith assures that we can have confidence in the presence of the Holy Spirit who permeates the process. Through contemplative reflection on personal experience enlightened by the scriptural revelation of God's ways with humans, the religious prophetically calls attention to that presence. This witness may not even involve much God-talk. It can simply be radiation of the inner joy and richness of one's life in the Spirit.

The reality is sometimes quite different. One sister recently spoke to me of her disillusionment with her community and with much anguish told me: "It all came to a head at our province assembly a few weeks ago. I looked around at several hundred sisters and all I saw were pale, drawn faces and no joy. They were all so tired looking. I then took a long look at myself and saw that I was the same. I don't want to live this way any longer."

RELIGIOUS LIVING IS HUMAN LIVING

To rediscover the life springs within, a therapeutic community such as the House of Affirmation, and, by extension, every religious community, should be a place where truth, reality, and faith prevail. The grace of healing is present in the community as a whole and in the individuals of the community. The same grace is given to the one who is healing and to the one who is being healed. All are called upon both to be healed and to be healers of others, no matter how much one may be personally hurting. It is my conviction that the grace of healing is given precisely at the growing edge of the personality. A person is healed when most exposed and vulnerable, and likewise performs the most graceful healing when the sore places are reaching out tenderly to touch another. When facade relates to facade, or even when facade relates to suffering humanity, there is a pretense of loving and caring. The head may be present to the other, but the heart is not. The grace of healing is mediated through the humanity of each person in the community.

In our special healing community, the House of Affirmation, the principal responsibility for creating the atmosphere, developing programs, etc., is with the staff. Each of us has come to this work through a personal odyssey of suffering, healing, change, and growth. We are willing to share this weakness, and it is our greatest strength. We are constantly being reminded of our own frailty and limitations. Yet, just as constantly, we discover the unfolding mystery of the action of God in our lives. This confidence in the strength and love of God gives us the willingness to risk feelings and responses of genuine love to the goodness of the other which is more important for healing than clinical skill alone. However, without the clinical expertise, we could easily lose our way in the problems that present themselves. Our task is to be both loving and professional.

We have found that in most religious, intellectual and even sometimes spiritual growth has outstripped emotional development. The characteristic defense mechanism of religious is intellectualization, in which feared emotional responses are cut off from and repressed by the intellect. Eventually the person becomes unable to feel anything at all. In our therapeutic program, the religious can discover and actualize creative potentialities through guided trial and error, and incorporate them into the whole process of growth. Thus, each individual comes to understand the uniqueness of his or her learning style and pace of growth. Nothing is forced or unnatural.

Another important dimension of our life together is the opportunity for men and women to live in the same community, and to learn to relate to one another as persons rather than as objects of fear or fantasy. This kind of living sometimes gives rise to reactions that are characteristic of delayed adolescence. When such feelings arise, they become the material for guided growth toward sexual maturity within the context of celibacy and its limits. We have found that celibacy as such is not the main problem of most who come to us. It is rather the lack of affirmation and affection which leads to problems in the area of sexuality. Only a small portion of those who have come through our program have left religious life.

GRACE IN NATURE FOR HEALING

We firmly believe that our therapy is a work of collaboration with the healing spirit of God in humanity. This work demands much reflection and contemplation of where and how God is present with his healing grace in each person. In this prayerful therapeutic process, the neurotic barriers to inner freedom in both the healer and healed are discovered, exposed, and removed. Growth in freedom and the consequent acceptance of increased responsibility demand deep faith in the incarnation, that God is among us in human flesh. Our goal, then, is to help religious with emotional disorders to achieve a balanced and integrated personhood, wherein all feelings are joyfully accepted and guided by the graced and gentle light of reason and will. To achieve this goal, we have provided a milieu where the process of conversion from denial to affirmation can be experienced. Our clients are becoming healed and are returning to creative service in the Church. Our files contain many letters from former residents and nonresidents, testifying to the permanency of the growth and changes that have occurred in their lives. The sad part is that frequently the communities and work situations have not changed. At the end of the course of treatment there is a renewed sense of the loving presence of God at deeper levels of the personality and an increased desire for prayer. It is not uncommon for a person to make a directed retreat prior to discharge with an affective responsiveness that was simply impossible before coming to us.

PREVENTION OF ILLNESS

I would like, finally, to make some observations about preventive mental health in religious community life. There is still among us a strong strain of moralism and idealistic perfectionism which compounds depressive guilt feelings and compulsive self-destructive behavior. We find that many of the neuroses we treat are aggravated by styles of spirituality and community life that encourage religious to be slavishly dependent, to intellectualize and mask the so-called negative feelings, and to try to be happy without giving and receiving genuine affection and warm love.

There is also a tendency to consume too much valuable energy with introspective community reorganization and constant revamping of structures. This inward-looking tendency stifles the apostolic spirit of reaching out to others in their need. Meetings upon meetings can have a very depressing effect on people. Moreover, religious particularly need to be reminded that they need to say "no" and to set limits on the demands that others make on their time and energy. The fine balance must be struck between helping others and being good to oneself. This means that religious professionals need to find outlets for creative recreation and hobbies, and to develop the ability to have fun and "waste time" enjoyably in ways that are more enriching than spending endless hours watching television or gossiping. Leisure time should be allowed for the development of friendships with persons of one's own choice, whether of the same or the other sex. For healthy living, time should also be set aside for contemplative reflection on one's own emotional and spiritual life in order fully to enjoy being alive and feeling. Prayer is time spent with the Lord, fostering an affective relationship with him. In an atmosphere of living trust, I can bring my other affective relationships to the Lord, so that they may develop under the guidance of his spirit without fear of reprisal or condemnation, since they also are God-given. A community goal should be to strive to discover and encourage every aspect of each other's total life situation that is truly life giving and affirming. Each person should be able to feel himself/herself as both a healer and as needing to be healed by others. Honest and frank conversation without censuring or judging is needed. There must be freedom to confront and challenge lovingly, in order to prevent an irresponsible permissiveness.

Thus our communities can become affirming when the persons in them feel that they are secure to be themselves, to make mistakes, and to find gentle forgiveness and deeply caring support one for the other. Our Church professes and proclaims that its roots and cornerstone are incarnate love. Yet, ironically, most of our religious patients come to us because there is a devastating lack of love in their lives.

CONCLUSION

In conclusion, I would like to state with gratitude that the work of the House of Affirmation has been abundantly blessed by God in the few years of its existence. While this might sound like excessive self-praise, this chapter was shared with our residents in a lively discussion before the final copy was made. They offered many perceptive observations and suggested changes, mostly where I had understated what they are experiencing of our healing ministry.

Church leaders have expressed their unanimous approval and support of our work. We have come upon many shoals which have nearly destroyed us. In each case we have been rescued by a presence that can only be called divine. Hence we rejoice and have great hope that our efforts will continue to be blessed, and that our service and experience will make a significant contribution to enhance the life of the whole Church.

PRAYER AND COMMUNITY

COMMUNITY AS A REFLECTION
OF THE TRINITY

In an earlier chapter entitled "Living in His Love," I discussed the notion that by saying we are created in the image of God, we are professing that we exist within the second person of the Trinity. In a spatial sense, that is where we are. When we consider this reality, we see that we have around us and share in the existence of the perfect community. The persons of the Trinity mirror a perfect image to each other of their glory, co-creative presence, beauty, and infinite love. We are called and destined to do likewise. Our purpose in life is to mirror to others who they are as seen by God through our eyes and vice versa. Of course, the more accurate, loving, and truthful the image reflected, the greater will we embody the creative action of the Trinity in our relationships.

It is important to reflect that material creation and humanity as the intelligent part of it do not stand outside

God, obeying his commands and giving him homage. God fashioned material creation to image back to him who he is. But we are not some fourth person of God doing in our way what the other three persons are doing. We exist in the second person and do what the Son does. Were it not for the Incarnation during which the second person of the Trinity took on humanity, such reflections would be beyond belief. As it is, we find ourselves situated where we individually assume the roles of the persons of the Trinity toward one another, that is, we co-create and love one another. Then, as the human community taken collectively, we image the Trinity back to itself.

What I am proposing is that through contemplation in faith we become aware of the spiritual dimension of our lives and relationships. I am not denying the human significance of life and love, but calling attention to the transcendent meaning that permeates the human.

This chapter reflects on one way our relationships in community can be contemplated. It is not my intention to expose how things ought to be, but rather to reflect on how they are whether we realize it or not. I would like to use the model of prayer as a way of understanding how our relationships with each other image the Trinitarian relations.

Our understanding of prayer is that it is normally a special kind of dialogue between a person and God or the angels or saints. There is, however, only one form of prayer that is unique and due only to God. That form is adoration. However, there are other forms of prayer that are not restricted or exclusive to our dialogue with God. In fact we can pray to one another. Perhaps by looking at how we pray to one another and our responses to such prayer, we can more faithfully reflect to God an image of the human community modeled on the divine community. To the extent that the human community reflects the divine, we fulfill the purpose of creation, which is to give glory to God. Glory is divine presence. So it seems that God wants to see evidence of his presence in material creation, particularly the human part of it. He wants to see an image of his creative goodness in the way humans express their creativity toward one another and the rest of material reality. Finally God wants to see the relations of the Trinity reflected in our relationships.

THANKSGIVING

In this chapter I will discuss three modes of prayer and how they relate to our experience of one another and God. The first mode is thanksgiving. The Psalmist exclaims: "I give you thanks that I am fearfully, wonderfully made; wonderful are your works" (139:14). This outburst of thanksgiving is the result of contemplating the goodness of his own being and of seeing God as the source of that being. Thanksgiving in its essence is the unqualified affirmation of existence. We can, in fact, address the words of the Psalmist to one another. By acknowledging the wonderfulness of the existence of the other, we are giving thanksgiving. All of God's creation and every person in it is worthy of such thanksgiving. This kind of thanksgiving reverences the existence of both the Creator and creation. By being grateful in this unqualified way, we are in fact sharing the attitude of the second person of the Trinity who is eternally grateful to the Father as the source of His own existence.

Even such a seemingly trivial act of thanksgiving as saying "thanks" when someone does a minor favor participates in eternal gratitude. It includes thanks that you are, thanks that you are able to be of service to me, and thanks that I am able to be of service to you. Again the Psalmist expresses this thanksgiving: "I will give thanks to you, O Lord, with all my heart; in the presence of the angels I will sing your praise; . . . and give thanks to your name, because of your kindness and your truth; . . . When I called, you answered me; you built up strength within me" (138:1-3).

In every case in which I am genuinely grateful to another and give thanks, I have indeed experienced some measure of truth and kindness, an answer to a call, and a strengthening. If I attend to it, I will always be able to discern these elements and, underlying them, love. Through all beneficence, however great or insignificant, is the presence of love. Responding to the actions of love with thanksgiving is a virtual recognition of the presence of the Holy Spirit. Thus thanksgiving is a prayer that is the appropriate response to the perceived creative action of love. While our giving thanks to one another most generally involves an attitude toward someone in response to a favor granted, it need not be thus limited. Our thanks to another implies gratitude to God for being Creator, for having created this person who has given a gift or favor, and for the love that prompted it.

Some of the conditions for the thanksgiving response that mirrors the relations of the Trinity are cited in the Psalm just quoted, in which the Psalmist is the recipient of kindness and truth, answers to calls, and the experience of strengthening. These are all human experiences. So when we experience kindness or truth within the other or within ourselves, there is cause for thanksgiving. Likewise whenever our calls have been answered by others or we feel ourselves being strengthened by others, we can thank them and, through them, be thanking God, the source of all that is.

It is entirely fitting that we should pray the prayer of thanksgiving toward one another. It is an attitude of unqualified joy in the wonderfulness of the existence of the other. In so doing for one another, we are imaging the attitude of the persons of the Trinity toward each other.

PRAISE

A second mode of prayer is praise. The attitude of praise is similar to that of thanksgiving. Praise is a qualified acknowledgment of the goodness of the other's actions. In giving praise to others, we mirror back to them the goodness in their achievements. We pay compliments to others in a wide variety of ways. It is very important to acknowledge the goodness of others as expressed through their deeds and accomplishments. Even as simple a prayer of praise as "you look good today" elicits in response the prayer of thanksgiving.

When we praise another, it is very important that we do so with sincerity, honesty, and truth. False or exaggerated praise undermines rather than affirms the other, and lack of praise does the same. Thus neither flattery nor indifference to the accomplishments of another can be a true embodiment of the relations of the Trinity. We can even praise the other through appropriate expressions of anger. Anger is generally a true reaction to deficiencies or failings in the other. It is a way of saying that we feel dismay at the imperfection we perceive in another's behavior insofar as it may injure or diminish us. Anger at least implies a caring, whereas the absence of anger can mean indifference. Scrip-

ture attributes anger to God in his dealings with his people
and vice versa. It is quite impossible that anger is any part
of the inner life of the Trinity. However, anger between
humans, when appropriate, can and does reflect to God
the embodiment of the divine community.

Jesus was lavish in his praise of the Father when he discerned the actions or presence of the Father in the world.
Yet he seems to have been quite sparing of praise for other
humans. At one point, "Jesus rejoiced in the Holy Spirit
and said: 'I offer you praise, O Father, Lord of heaven and
earth, because what you have hidden from the learned and
the clever you have revealed to the merest children. Yes,
Father, you have graciously willed it so'" (Luke 10:21).
Jesus saw that the merest children were receiving the word
of God, that they were understanding the message with
faith while the clever were not. As Jesus contemplated the
reality that some heard and some did not, and as he
thought about what kind of people they were respectively,
he discerned the active presence of the Father and gave him
praise. Thus prayer of praise is appropriate whenever the
presence of God is discerned, especially when responding
to the good news of salvation. Likewise, whenever the
goodness of another's actions is appreciated, praise is due
both to the human agent of the goodness and to its ultimate source.

Scripture offers very few examples of Jesus praising people. But after Peter made his profession of faith in Jesus as
the Messiah (Matt. 16:17), Jesus said, "Blest are you,
Simon son of Jonah! No mere man has revealed this to
you, but my heavenly Father." In thus blessing, or praising, Peter, Jesus again acknowledged the presence and activity of the Father. So once again there is a dual aspect to

the praise. Jesus praised the Father because he had chosen Peter for that revelation, and Jesus praised Peter as well because he was open to receive it.

Prayer of praise as we express praise to one another is a co-operative dimension of our lives in community. It indeed images and reflects to the Trinity the way they relate to each other. We need then to praise one another after the model of the prayer of the Trinity: "This is my beloved Son on whom my favor rests" (Matt. 17:5) and "I offer you praise, O Father, Lord of heaven and earth. . . ." (Luke 10:21). When we praise one another's good actions and deplore the bad, with an awareness that we are reflecting God's attitudes, our human community proclaims that it indeed does recognize that it is formed in the image of the divine.

PETITION

The third mode of prayer is petition. Again we can use prayer as a way of defining and understanding our relationships with one another. Prayer of petition is the presentation of needs and the acknowledgement of dependency on one another. We simply are neither self-sufficient nor complete within ourselves. Prayer of petition, the asking that our needs be fulfilled, is an admission of our poverty. We need others to share themselves and their goods with us and vice versa in order to fill up and complete us. A request granted again stimulates prayer of thanksgiving and praise.

Jesus in his need frequently petitions the Father. Moreover, his place now is at the right hand of the Father, constantly interceding on our behalf. Yet our experience confirms that most of our needs are met when we petition other persons and the requests are granted. The bounty of God comes to us for the most part through other human beings. It follows, then, that asking and receiving from one another is a way of bonding ourselves together in dependency and in generous love that is a characteristic of the persons of the Trinity.

When we petition one another, two of the greatest virtues, humility and charity, are activated. Charity is the love of the good of the other; response to petition is loving fulfillment of the other's needs. This charity is quite different from the response of the "pleaser" who does not know personal limits and is afraid to say no out of fear or guilt. Sometimes a no to a request is the truly loving and creative response.

Jesus often petitioned people to fill his needs. For example, he asked the Samaritan woman in John 4:7 to give him a drink. Yet he was aware of and reflected on the fact that there are different levels of thirst and that while the woman was answering his prayer on one level, it was she who needed to pray for a drink on another level. All the levels of dependency are an admission and symbol of our radical poverty. Simply stated, we are completely dependent on God for salvation. We need to petition for this ultimate gift constantly. It takes humility to ask another for something. With practice and contemplative reflection, we will grow in confidence and trust that God will meet all our needs, including being with him in eternity.

In our life in community we should be aware that much more is going on than immediately meets the eye. Since we exist in the image of God, we need to see how we not only reflect to God his goodness by our individual perfection, but also how our interrelatedness and the bonds of our mutual dependence reflect a community of love to the paradigm of such community, the Holy Trinity.

AFFIRMATION

In conclusion, I would like to add that what I have been speaking of is affirmation. Affirmation is the co-creation we are all called upon to share with God. We are in a real sense creators of one another. It is almost as if God had created the human person in existence and left it to other humans to bring that person to the fullness of his or her potentialities. The work of creation is always unfinished, and it cannot be finished until we affirm one another into that completeness of the work God has begun. In a special sense, we stand in the role of God toward one another. As such, then, it is fitting that we express prayer toward one another that we be brought together to become what in fact we truly are, the image of the Trinity.

LIVING COMMUNITY

COMMUNITY AS SHARED LIFE

In my previous chapter, "Community as a Reflection of the Trinity," I proposed that our community life reflects the relationships of the persons of the Trinity. I used the model of three kinds of prayer to describe the affirming interactions we have with one another. In fact, from the faith point of view, we do indeed, in various degrees, whether conscious or not, live out the prayer of Jesus, "I pray . . . that all may be one as you, Father, are in me, and I in you; . . . so that your love for me may live in them and I may live in them" (John 17: 20-21, 26). We are included in the inner life of the Trinity by virtue of our baptism, and thus our interactions with each other have a quality and meaning analogous to those of the Trinity.

Now the question arises concerning our lived experience of this unity. How do we in fact experience this common unity—community—and how can we enhance our consciousness of it? In this chapter, I discuss how in our community life, united as we are in the body of Christ, the experience of one is the experience of all. Perhaps, put more simply, life is shared on all levels. I am not saying that life and experiences *should* be communicated and shared among members of the community; I am saying that they inevitably are shared. There are many ways to communicate both verbally and nonverbally. When I am living in extended proximity with others, I am sending out to them clues and signals about what is going on in my life. The signals may be ambiguous because I may be trying to mask what is happening in and to me, or the listener may not be sufficiently sensitive to understand my message; but I am always saying something about myself and my experience.

If our communities are to be places in which we continue to grow and develop in our humanity as well as in our life of contemplation and faith, it is obvious that the quality of communication must be as clear and as open as possible. In fact, lack of communication is the most common source of difficulty in our communities. One of the deepest human yearnings is to be lovingly understood by another person. We often express our fulfillment of that yearning by saying to the other person, "With you I can really be myself." When no such person is available, our need is felt as a hungry desire, and we often say, "I wish there were someone in my life who really knows me and cares about me." Concurrent with this longing is the intense fear we all have of being judged and condemned by another. It is my experience that many good, committed religious people are interiorly paralyzed because they are caught between these conflicting desires. They want to be lovingly understood, but that means they must consciously reveal themselves. If they reveal themselves as they are, they run the risk of being judged and rejected.

BALANCE OF CLOSENESS AND DISTANCE

I have reflected in previous chapters that human community is an incarnate image of the prototypical community, the Trinity. However, precisely because it is incarnate, our living together will not be perfectly heavenly. In order for human community to effectively satisfy our human needs, it must be a relatively stable set of relationships. Constantly changing the place where we live, the work we do, and the people with whom we live makes development of the continuity necessary for mutual trust difficult. Another requirement of community is that its members are committed to the same general values and goals. This similarity does not mean that all think exactly alike or assign the same personal value in every circumstance. That would be a monotonous uniformity. Healthy differences of opinion on even relatively serious matters is the stuff from which mature adult relationships grow. An attitude of "if you don't think like me, you don't belong to me" is destructive of community and is not even Christian.

On the other side of the spectrum, a community can resemble a group of individuals who share little although they are gathered under the same roof. An airport terminal houses such a gathering. All persons are there in busy pursuit of a common goal, to catch an airplane. Unfortunately, too many communities and rectories resemble such terminals in which people busily pursuing individual projects happen to intersect. But for community to be the kind of place wherein people grow and develop in all the dimensions of their lives, it must provide stability, continuity, and time shared together.

SHARING FEELINGS BRINGS CLOSENESS AND TRUST

It should also be noted that a community is itself an organism that has a life and process of its own. In this respect, it is similar to a family. Families have a genealogy, a history, operating rules, a self-image, tasks to perform, an economy, and sets of values. Families function effectively for the well-being of their members when all these aspects of family life become the common concern of all to the extent that each is mature enough to participate in and assume responsibility for them. A community that simply provides the basic necessities of life in a ready-made fashion such that its members can function in their apostolic tasks without temporal distractions does not satisfy the deeper needs of the people living in it.

Every human being, each one of us, has a very profound need to experience that we matter, that in personally significant ways our life makes a difference to someone else. We need to be included in someone else's life and to include others in our own. I do not believe that our most significant relationships must necessarily be within the community where we live. But if only a minimum of sharing exists among those who live together, we might certainly ask how much such a grouping deserves to be called a community.

I mentioned earlier that people who live together inevitably share with one another what is going on inside each. Ideally, the level of conscious and explicit sharing among some or all members of a community should match the level of nonverbal sharing. When, for example, someone is angry and is acting in a grumpy way, such behavior and attitude affects everyone who comes in contact with him or her. If such behavior is accompanied by denials that anything is wrong, communication breaks down and confusion results. The person thus suffering remains isolated with his or her feelings and can become withdrawn or depressed. Whatever a person is carrying around inside, even though it is thought to be hidden and private, is by that fact already a community concern. It is then the responsibility of the community as well as the individual to seek to explicitly resolve the issue. The level of mutual trust and courage that the risk of such sharing and working through requires is quite high. Whenever risk is involved, we can expect anxiety, fear, and defensiveness to also be present. I believe that there is material here for asceticism, self-denial, and the mortification that is necessary for the true practice of humility and charity.

I have just given the example of a person in community who is communicating angry feelings. The same need to make explicit what is going on inside applies to the whole range of human experiences. The life of community is immeasurably enriched when joys and successes as well as griefs or failures are shared. If we can truly delight in the happiness of one another, our own happiness is increased. If an event in one member's life is personally important and yet no one else considers it as important, the member might feel a sense of loneliness and alienation or even resentment. Even joy can be very quickly dampened when there is no one who cares to share it.

In a therapeutic community such as the House of Affirmation, a very conscious effort is made to share personal experiences. Some of these experiences are from the past, and some are contemporary. Attention is given to each person's reactions to what is happening either in the life of another individual or to something of general community concern. It is often quite surprising how much richness of feeling is generated concerning almost every circumstance. When encouragement and opportunity are provided for such sharing, it becomes abundantly evident that no event in any person's life can be considered trivial. Moreover, when the event is shared and further reflections and reactions are elicited, the community itself becomes more unified, and the individuals in it grow and deepen in awareness and sensitivity. Of course, it is impossible in busy communities and rectories to pay such concentrated attention to the inner lives of members. The point is that our experience shows that there is a great wealth of material in everyone. Unfortunately, these treasures are all too often locked away beyond even the conscious possession of the persons themselves.

COMPENSATION MECHANISMS

A wide variety of mechanisms come into play when the inner life is blocked. These range from severe neurosis to mildly compulsive character traits. I would like to discuss one mechanism that we frequently see in religious professionals. It is observed in a person who develops a particular skill that he or she then uses to support a weak self-image.

A sense of personal importance is one of life's basic needs. Therefore, all human beings in one way or another need to have something they can point to and say to themselves that at least in this one respect they are important and worthwhile. Ideally, of course, this sense of personal value comes from childhood and not from a drive for achievement. If our earliest convictions are that we are valued for ourselves, that we belong to someone, and that our lives are significant and matter to another, we will generally carry these convictions with us all our lives. However, if somehow these personal convictions of worth are missing, most of life thereafter will be spent trying to accomplish something that will bring the needed attention and recognition. When our deeds and achievements and, as a result, we ourselves are not recognized, we experience a great sense of personal deflation. It is as if a stage actor had put on his best performance and no one applauded. If no one in the actor's life loves him independently of his performance, the effect can be personally shattering.

Most people who are thus driven to prove themselves normally develop personal insurance against criticism or failure. They seldom take a risk or make a decision to which anyone could possibly take exception. Sometimes, however, they develop such an expertise in some area of accomplishment that they can tell themselves, even if no one else does, that at least they are good at something. Such compensation rarely accomplishes its purpose. Inside, the person remains alone, hiding behind a facade of competence. Often the person trapped within is unaware of the inner pain and isolation. The busyness and intensity of energy devoted to achievement effectively blocks the inner awareness. It usually takes a personal crisis or crash of some sort to bring the hidden to light. A person is indeed fortunate if at that time there is a loving friend to stand by, since efforts at self-affirmation never succeed.

SPIRITUAL AND PSYCHIC PATTERNS

Our spiritual lives and relationship with God generally follow the pattern of our psychic structure. In the situation we have been discussing, namely, the person who attempts to compensate for insecurity through achievement, the same dynamic will characterize his or her spiritual life. It is not uncommon to see people who seem to be trying to prove to God that they are good. The image of God that they project is one of a stern taskmaster who never seems to be satisfied or pleased. The reality is, of course, that their own critical observing selves are never satisfied. Another form of spiritualization that is a compensation for a low sense of personal worth is to make God the sole and exclusive affirmer. In this situation, God becomes the substitute for affirming human relationships. Nobody else may love me, but I know that at least God does. I know my life matters to him, and I can hang on to this truth when all else fails. Normally, this form of spirituality will fail in time because it is founded on an intellectualized truth rather than felt experience. It is simply another form of talking oneself into good feelings. It is like the desperate orphan telling herself that she knows her parents love her even though they abandoned her and have not returned.

CONCLUSION

I think it is plain from this discussion how important community and personal relationships are in our lives. Our spiritual lives and our psychic and emotional lives are very close and constantly overflow from one to the other. Our religious communities, if they are to be incarnations of Christ's very real and human love, need to attend to the inner lives of each of their members. Since the inner happenings will manifest themselves anyway, in indirect and often destructive ways, means must be developed and maintained for the regular expression and working through of these feelings. Such means give each person the conviction that what is happening in and to him or her is significant not only to himself or herself but to others as well. It is a great sin of omission, one that actually kills the spirit, when what is important to one is not recognized and affirmed by others, especially in a religious community that is founded explicitly for the purpose of practicing such charity. It is literally true that we can wipe ourselves out and wipe out one another through benign neglect and inattention. On the other hand, we can greatly increase and expand the richness and vitality of our inner lives by sharing and incorporating the experiences of others.